GW00471755

Let's Braai

Carmen Niehaus

I'm privileged in that every day my life is enriched with wonderful colleagues, assistants and photographers with whom I spend many hours in the kitchen and studio, people who like to share their ideas, come up with plans and love sharing a joke. I again relied on the *YOU* team for the fantastic photographs in *YOU Let's Braai*. Thank you, Daleen, Bernice and David.

Let's Braai

Carmen Niehaus

I would like to thank my family who agreed to pose as models: dad Carel and mom Jo van Zyl; Lodewyk, HW and Hanje Niehaus; Johan, Mientjie and Boet Mouton (pity CP and Lize were writing exams); Johan, Hannalize, Salomé, Jo and Carel van Zyl; Potgieter, Ronel, Marthine, Bridget and CP van Zyl; Rikus, Aletta, SJ, Van Zyl, Rikus, young Ebeth Groenewald and mom Suzie Niehaus. Sisteen Louw, thank you for all the wonderful food we could tuck into on the flat rock. I would also like to thank youngsters Wilbur Ndaba, Bradley-Owen Basson and Jean-Lee Basson who grew up on the farm for braving the wind to pose for a picture. Many thanks to Daleen van der Merwe for preparing the dishes for photography and her endless inspiration, knowledge and quick hands in the test kitchen; Priscilla Petersen for her indispensable help in the kitchen, Bernice van der Merwe for styling the wonderful photographs, sourcing props and her creativity that has made each photograph unique and stylish; David Briers for his pictures of not only the food but also his lifestyle pictures for which he sacrificed many a weekend. I would also like to thank Vanessa Holies who had to make literally thousands of copies of recipes; Tania de Kock of publishers Human & Rousseau, who managed the entire project – thank you for your support and input and for ensuring that we made the deadlines. And thank you Petal Palmer of PETALDESIGN for the beautiful book design and your enthusiasm.

Family picture on pg 78/79: Preparation of dishes by Sisteen Louw of Clanwilliam Butchery; wine supplied by Johan van Zyl and Goue Vallei Wines.

Cover: Whole mealies (pg 179); vegetable kebabs (pg 182) and T-bone steak with herb butter (pg 34).

Photography: David Briers. Styling: Carmen Niehaus.

First published in 2007 by Human & Rousseau
A division of NB Publishers (Pty) Ltd
40 Heerengracht, Cape Town 8000

Publisher	Tania de Kock
Editor	Joy Clack
Design	PETALDESIGN
Photography	David Briers
Recipe preparation and styling	Daleen van der Merwe and Bernice van der Merwe

Reproduction by Resolution Colour Pty (Ltd), Cape Town, RSA
Printed and bound by Tien Wah (Pte) Ltd, Singapore

ISBN-10	0-7981-4873-X
ISBN-13	978-0-7981-4873-3

Copyright © published edition
Human & Rousseau (2007)
Copyright © text Carmen Niehaus (2007)

No part of this book may be reproduced or transmitted in any form or by any electronic or mechanical means, including photocopying and recording, or by any other information storage or retrieval system, without written permission from the publisher.

Accessories supplied courtesy of Enamel, Heartworks, Loft Living, Louis Naude Messe, Die Gieter, Alison's for Flowers and Antiques and L'Orangerie.

Contents

Mastering the art of braaiing   **6**

Snacks and starters   **16**

Succulent steaks   **24**

Mouthwatering venison   **40**

Versatile pork   **54**

Melt-in-the-mouth lamb   **70**

Skewers, burgers and boerewors   **86**

Wholesome chicken   **102**

Fresh from the sea: fish and seafood   **124**

Heavenly breads and other bakes   **148**

Healthy salads and vegetables   **162**

Sweet temptations   **192**

Index   **206**

'Every braai enthusiast has his or her own secrets for turning out a perfectly char-grilled steak. And when it comes to lighting the fire there are so many rituals you'll be caught in the crossfire if you were to take sides.'

mastering the art of Braaiing

One thing I do know is that it takes time and practice and experimenting with food to become skilled at braaiing. You must be able to tell how hot the fire is and know when to raise or lower the grid, add or remove coals and when to remove the meat or baste and turn it just one more time. I've also included a few ideas for basic marinades, rubs, sauces and pestos, which will add instant flavour to any dish.

GENERAL TECHNIQUES

The success of a braai depends mainly on the heat of the coals. They must be hot enough to seal the meat rapidly so the flavour and juices are retained but not so hot that the outside is burnt to a cinder before the inside is done. The degree of heat also depends on the kind of meat, the cut and the size of the cut.

ON AN OPEN FIRE

- If using briquettes ensure they are burnt out and covered with a thin grey layer before you put the meat on the grid.
- A wood fire is ready only once the flames have died down and you're left with a heap of glowing coals.
- If you need cooler coals wait a little until the worst heat has dissipated. Alternatively, set the grid high above the coals and lower it a little later.
- Large cuts of meat can also be successfully cooked over the coals: simply cover the cut with a dome lid or a sheet of aluminium foil folded double in the shape of a dome to trap the heat inside so it resembles an oven or kettle braai.

IN A KETTLE BRAAI

A kettle braai is similar to a convection oven so just about anything you cook in an ordinary oven can be cooked in a kettle braai. This means when you have a braai you no longer have to stick to just chops and kebabs as a kettle braai is also ideal for doing larger meat cuts.

The success of using a kettle braai depends largely on how skilled you are at using the air vents to control the heat. Briquettes are used to make a fire in a kettle braai. The most important thing to remember is that the briquettes must be completely burnt out before you put the meat on the grid – it takes 20–25 minutes. There are two methods of braaiing in a kettle braai: the direct method and the indirect method.

DIRECT METHOD

This method is suitable for chops, kebabs and vegetables. It works like a conventional braai where the burnt-out coals are spread evenly on the coal grid. The meat is first sealed by rapidly searing it on both sides on the preheated grid. The meat is then covered with the lid and left to cook. Turn once halfway during the braai time.

INDIRECT METHOD

Any meat cut that needs longer than 30 minutes to cook, such as whole pieces of meat or chicken, must be cooked using the indirect method, which is similar to oven-roasting.

Arrange the burnt-out briquettes (coals) on both sides of the grid and put a drip tray in the middle. The tray will catch all the rendered fat. (For lengthy braai times, add a little water to the drip tray.) Place the braai grid on top and arrange the meat on the grid so that it lies above the drip tray and between the two heaps of coals. Cover with the lid and only open the braai to add more coals, brush the meat with marinade or check it for doneness. (Ensure you have enough extra coals on hand to replace the burnt-out coals.)

AIR VENTS: The more you open the air vents the hotter the coals will be, so keep a close eye on the vents, opening and closing them as required.

TIP: Put the meat on a wire rack inside an aluminium foil container to catch the rendered fat and juices. Cover the kettle braai with the lid and open only to test for doneness or to add more coals.

ON A GAS BRAAI

First heat the grid by setting all the burners on high. Adjust them to the required braai temperature after about 10 minutes.

Put the meat on the grid, seal it rapidly on both sides and cover with the lid. Braai until done.

When cooking large cuts over gas, switch off the middle burner directly under the meat so heat is provided by the outer burners only (this is similar to the indirect method for a kettle braai).

MARINADES

WHY MARINADE?

Marinade not only adds flavour to the meat, the acidity in the marinade also helps to tenderise it.

Some marinades burn quite easily so pat the meat dry before putting it on the braai. Set the grid higher and turn the meat frequently.

HOW LONG SHOULD THE MEAT BE MARINATED?

This depends on the kind of meat and the size of the cut. Large cuts can be left to marinate in marinade from a few hours to a day or two at most. Don't leave them too long or the meat will become 'floury'. Chicken and venison are ideal for marinating. Chops and steaks are best as is, without any extraneous flavours to mask the natural flavour of the meat, but a little braai sauce will enhance them. Fish is naturally juicy and delicately flavoured so it is only marinated to impart a specific flavour, such as Cajun or Thai. Make incisions in the meat or fish to enable the flavours to penetrate.

HOW TO MARINADE MEAT

Arrange the meat in a single layer in a shallow non-metallic dish. Pour over the marinade, ensuring the meat is well coated. Cover and leave the meat or chicken to marinate in the marinade for about 1 hour or about 30 minutes for fish. Turn once.

TIP: Baste with the marinade from time to time. Don't put the cooked meat in the remaining uncooked marinade – the marinade in which the raw meat was marinated contains bacteria that could make you ill. If you want to serve leftover marinade with the meat, first bring it to the boil.

Basic marinade

This marinade is easy to prepare and can be adapted for lamb or pork chops or for chicken or beef.

Blend the ingredients and adjust them depending on the kind of meat (below).

90 ml oil
30 ml lemon juice or white
   wine vinegar
2 cloves garlic, crushed

MAKES 120 ML.

FOR LAMB: Prepare the basic marinade. Add a pinch of cumin, 15 ml chopped fresh mint or oregano, 30 ml chopped sun-dried tomatoes and 30 ml chopped fresh basil.

FOR CHICKEN OR PORK: Prepare the basic marinade. Add 15 ml tomato purée, 15 ml soy sauce, chopped fresh coriander and grated fresh ginger to taste. OR add 15 ml honey and 15 ml prepared mustard.

WITH ROSEMARY: Use this marinade for lamb, beef, pork or chicken. Prepare the basic marinade. Add the leaves of 2 sprigs of rosemary and 2 ml freshly ground black pepper.

WITH MUSTARD: Use this marinade for lamb, beef, chicken or fish. Prepare the basic marinade. Add 30 ml Dijon mustard and 1 chopped onion or shallot.

WITH CITRUS: For chicken or pork. Prepare the basic marinade. Add the juice and grated zest of 3 oranges, the zest of 1 lemon, and 30 ml each chopped chives and parsley.

Spicy yoghurt marinade

This fragrant marinade is ideal for chicken, fish or lamb.

250 ml plain yoghurt or buttermilk
2 cloves garlic, crushed
2 cm piece fresh ginger, finely grated
juice of ½ lemon
5 ml ground cumin

5 ml ground coriander
2 ml ground cardamom
2 ml cayenne pepper
2 ml salt
45 ml chopped fresh mint (optional)

Mix all the ingredients and pour into a screw-top jar. Store in the fridge until needed. (This marinade can be stored for up to one week.) *[pg 10, top]*

MAKES 250 ML.

Cajun marinade

Use this hot and spicy marinade for anything from fish and prawns to chicken, lamb or beef.

15 ml ground allspice
15 ml cayenne pepper
15 ml black peppercorns, crushed
10 ml ground cinnamon

100 ml tomato purée
100 ml sunflower oil
15 ml balsamic vinegar
2 cloves garlic, crushed

Mix all the ingredients and pour into a screw-top jar. Store in the fridge for up to 2 weeks. *[pg 10, centre]*

MAKES 200 ML.

Chinese marinade

Use for beef, pork, chicken or fish.

30 ml rice wine vinegar
60 ml soy sauce
15 ml sesame oil
30 ml honey

2 cm piece fresh ginger, grated
2 cloves garlic, crushed
5 ml five-spice powder

Mix all the ingredients. Pour into a screw-top jar and store in the fridge until needed. (This marinade can be stored for 1–2 weeks.) *[pg 10, bottom]*

MAKES 130 ML.

chutney and tomato braai sauce

Brush lamb, pork or ribs with this sauce while braaiing.

125 ml sunflower oil
60 ml tomato sauce
60 ml chutney
5 ml curry powder
2 ml turmeric
30 ml apricot jam

Blend all the ingredients, pour into a container and store in the fridge until needed. (This marinade can be stored for up to 2 weeks.) *[pg 11, top]*

MAKES 250 ML.

Wine marinade

500 ml white wine, or 250 ml white
    wine and 250 ml chicken stock
100 ml tomato sauce
5 ml Tabasco sauce
100 ml Worcestershire sauce
5 ml paprika
100 ml smooth apricot jam
2 cloves garlic, crushed
2 onions, finely chopped
5 ml dried thyme
5 ml mustard powder
125 ml sunflower oil

Blend all the ingredients, pour into a screw-top jar and store in the fridge until needed. Marinate chicken pieces in the marinade. Bring any leftover marinade to the boil and simmer well. Freeze until required. *[pg 11, centre]*

MAKES 800 ML.

versatile curry sauce

The sauce acts as a preservative and meat, such as chops or sosaties, marinated in it will last longer, making it ideal if you're short of space in the freezer.

4 large onions, sliced
250 ml water
1 small chilli, seeded and finely
    chopped (optional)
25 ml sugar
25 ml curry powder
10 ml salt
3 ml freshly ground black pepper
5 ml turmeric
2 ml ground ginger
25 ml ground coriander
50 ml apricot jam
500 ml brown vinegar

Bring all the ingredients, except the vinegar, to the boil. Reduce the heat and simmer for 5 minutes. Add the vinegar and leave to cool. Store in the fridge and use as needed. Marinate meat in the sauce for at least 4 hours. *[pg 11, bottom]*

MAKES 750 ML.

RUBS AND OTHER SPICE MIXES

Instead of marinating meat or vegetables in marinades you can rub them with a fragrant dry spice mix. Herbs and spices are ground together to make a delicious mixture for seasoning meat, fish or chicken before it goes on the braai.

TIP: Sprinkle the mixture over vegetables or mix it with breadcrumbs and sprinkle it over, for instance, chicken, as a crust. Alternatively, blend it with oil or yoghurt to make a runny paste and use the mixture as a marinade.

Lemon and herb rub

Mix 4 large chopped cloves garlic, grated rind of 1 lemon, 10 ml finely chopped fresh rosemary, 5 ml dried basil, 3 ml salt, 3 ml dried thyme, and 3 ml freshly ground black pepper. Store in an airtight container in the fridge. Ideal for fish or pork. *[pg 12, top]*

Braai rub

Use this rub for braai cuts such as leg of lamb or pork, pork neck or even a whole chicken. Add oil just before using if you prefer working with a paste.

Mix 10 ml paprika, 15 ml brown sugar, 5 ml ground cumin, 5 ml mustard powder, 10 ml freshly ground black pepper, and 5 ml garlic salt. Store in an airtight container.

Texas rub

This rather hot rub will add flavour to beef, pork and lamb.

Mix 1 crushed clove garlic, 5 ml mustard seeds, 5 ml salt, 5 ml chilli powder, 5 ml cayenne pepper, 5 ml paprika, 3 ml ground coriander, and 3 ml ground cumin. Store in an airtight container in the fridge.

Spicy Moroccan rub

Use this fragrant mix for rubbing meat or sprinkling over vegetables such as pumpkin and cabbage before roasting. Also excellent stirred into couscous.

Mix 5 ml paprika, 5 ml ground nutmeg, 5 ml ground cumin, 5 ml ground coriander, 2 ml ground allspice, 2 ml ground ginger, 1 ml cayenne pepper, and 1 ml ground cinnamon. Store in an airtight container. *[pg 12, bottom]*

TIP: Add the grated zest of a lemon and a chopped clove garlic if desired.

Indonesian spice mix

Roll chicken breasts, fish fillets or pork steaks in this mix before frying lightly in heated oil in a pan over the coals.

Mix 5 ml cayenne pepper, 5 ml ground cumin, 5 ml ground coriander, 5 ml ground cardamom seeds, 150 ml sesame seeds, and 150 ml cake flour. Store in an airtight container.

Cajun spice mix

Rub chicken, steak or fish with this fragrant mix before char-grilling.

Blend in a food processor: 30 ml salt, 10 ml cayenne pepper, 10 ml paprika, 15 ml dried onion flakes, 5 ml dried garlic flakes, 15 ml finely ground peppercorns, 5 ml peri-peri powder, 10 ml dried oregano, 5 ml dried thyme, 5 ml dried basil, 5 ml brown sugar, and a pinch of mustard powder. Store in an airtight container and use as needed.

NORTH AFRICAN RUBS

Chermoula

This paste is fragrant rather than hot. Mix with about 80 ml oil or yoghurt and spread over any meat, chicken or fish.

Place 125 ml chopped fresh coriander, 125 ml chopped fresh parsley, 4 finely crushed cloves garlic, 30 ml grape vinegar, 80 ml lemon juice, 2 ml ground cumin, 7 ml paprika, 2 ml chilli powder, and a pinch of salt in a food processor and blend until fine. Store in a glass jar in the fridge for up to 1 week.

MAKES 100 ML.

Harissa

Harissa is a hot North African paste used to flavour meat, tajine (stew) and couscous. It's especially good rubbed into lamb before putting it on the fire.

Cover 125 g chopped dried chillies with boiling water and soak for 1 hour. Drain and blend with 20 ml dried mint, 20 ml ground cumin, 20 ml ground coriander, 5 ml caraway seeds, and 10 ml chopped garlic in a food processor. Add 60 ml olive oil and blend to a paste. Store in the fridge for about 6 months. *[pg 13, bottom]*

PESTO AND OTHER SPREADS

Feta, almond and paprika pesto

Blend 100 g almond flakes, 40 g grated Parmesan cheese, 2 rounds crumbled feta cheese, 5–10 ml paprika, 80 ml chopped fresh parsley, and 180 ml olive oil in a food processor.

MAKES ABOUT 250 ML.

Coriander pesto

Place 125 ml fresh coriander, 60 ml fresh parsley, 20 ml pine nuts or almonds, 100 ml grated Parmesan cheese, 5 ml finely chopped garlic, 30 ml lemon or lime juice, and 125 ml olive oil in a food processor and blend together. *[pg 15]*

MAKES ABOUT 250 ML.

TIPS:

- Stir pesto into pasta, add extra cheese and serve with braaied meat.
- Mix pesto with mayonnaise and stir into potato salad.
- Spread pesto over bruschetta, scatter feta cheese on top and serve as a snack.
- Spread pizza bases or bread dough with pesto instead of tomato sauce and top with your favourite ingredients.
- Mix pesto with breadcrumbs and sprinkle over chicken.
- Mix pesto with ricotta cheese and use as a stuffing for mushrooms or peppers before roasting them over the coals.

Chimichurri

This Argentinian parsley sauce is delicious with spicy roast leg of lamb and is also a good alternative to pesto.

Blend in a food processor: 30 ml white vinegar, 50 ml sunflower oil, 45 ml chopped fresh flat-leaf parsley, 5 ml chopped fresh oregano, 2 crushed cloves garlic, 5 ml paprika, and 1 seeded and chopped green chilli. Spoon into a clean jar and chill overnight. *[pg 13, top]*

MAKES ABOUT 125 ML.

Onion marmalade

Sauté 6 onions (sliced into thick rings) in olive oil until soft. Add 150 ml red wine vinegar, 3 bay leaves, 2 whole cloves, and 125 ml sugar. Bring to the boil, then reduce the heat and simmer until all the liquid has been absorbed. Add 100 ml red wine and reduce until syrupy.

coriander pesto

'Set a table on the stoep and serve a selection of nibbles with pre-dinner drinks so your guests can watch the last of the sun's rays disappearing below the horizon. Then it won't matter at all when you serve the main course.'

snacks and Starters

Do it the Spanish way with tapas (a selection of snacks in bowls) or make an Italian platter of antipasti. You can also make bruschetta (toasted Italian bread with toppings), tartlets or cocktail sticks. Alternatively, make a platter with a variety of loaves and spreads (see the section on bread, pg 149). Or simply put out bowls of nuts and/or biltong and droëwors to stave off the hunger pangs.

TAPAS

Prepare a variety of snacks beforehand and set them out on the table with freshly baked bread. Here are a few ideas.

Deep-fried calamari

Cut calamari steaks into strips. Combine 250 ml cake flour, 250 ml desiccated coconut and 125 ml coarse mealie meal until crumbly. Season with salt and freshly ground black pepper. Roll the calamari in the flour mixture until completely coated, and then deep-fry in oil until golden brown. Drain on paper towel and serve with fresh lime or lemon wedges. *[pg 18, bottom]*

VARIATION: Mix 5 ml paprika and 2 ml cayenne pepper with the cake flour instead of coconut and mealie meal.

Prawns

Defrost shelled and deveined prawns in cold water. Drain and fry in hot oil with chopped garlic and chilli until they turn pink. Drizzle with lime juice and serve with coriander pesto (pg 14) mixed with a little extra olive oil.

Chicken nuggets

Snip off the tips of chicken wings and cut through at the joints. Sprinkle with plenty of soy sauce and roll each piece in flour seasoned with paprika, salt and freshly ground black pepper. Fry in a little hot oil until brown on the outside. Cover the pan, reduce the heat and braise until done. Serve hot. *[pg 18, top]*

Sweet 'n sour chicken wings

Brush the chicken wings with any sweet 'n sour sauce and braai until done. Make a dip with 150 ml sour cream, 50 g crumbled blue cheese and 45 ml mayonnaise. Serve with the chicken wings.

Chicken liver and bacon rolls

Season chicken livers with salt and freshly ground black pepper and fry in hot oil until just done. Wrap in bacon rashers and secure with cocktail sticks. Grill in the oven or over the coals until done. *[pg 18, centre]*

Braaied mussels

Arrange mussels on the half-shell in an oven pan. Mix 2 chopped cloves garlic, 15 ml melted butter, 15 ml olive oil, 15 ml lemon juice, 3 ml salt, 5 ml chopped fresh oregano, and 1 ml lemon pepper and sprinkle over the mussels. Heat under the oven grill for about 5 minutes until hot and done. *[pg 19, top]*

Fried halloumi

Cut halloumi cheese into slices and dust with flour. Heat a little oil in a pan and fry until golden brown on both sides. Serve with lemon wedges. *[pg 19, bottom]*

TIP: Make individual salads for guests using halloumi cheese: Arrange rocket on a plate, top with a slice of fried halloumi cheese, drizzle with Eastern salad dressing (pg 165) and stack a few slivers of ham, such as prosciutto or Parma or Black Forest ham, on top.

Roasted brinjal

Halve smallish brinjals lengthways. Cut notches in the brinjal halves and rub salt in generously. Leave to stand for 10–15 minutes. Pat dry with paper towels and arrange on a baking sheet. Drizzle generously with olive oil and scatter chopped garlic and fresh thyme on top. Roast for 15–20 minutes at 200 °C or until soft. Pile feta cheese on top and heat in the oven until melted.

Roasted tomatoes

Use vine-ripened tomatoes if available, otherwise use plum tomatoes. Halve the tomatoes, and then sprinkle with salt, chopped garlic, freshly ground black pepper, and olive oil. Arrange on a baking sheet and bake in a cool oven until the skins begin to wrinkle. Sprinkle with balsamic vinegar just before serving. *[pg 19, centre]*

Salad bowls

Make individual bowls of salad for guests with salad greens such as rocket, endive and mizuna. Slice nectarines or fresh pears and pile on top (roast beforehand if desired). Crumble blue cheese on top and moisten with mustard vinaigrette (pg 164). Scatter toasted walnuts or sunflower seeds on top.

TIP: See section on salads (pg 163) for more ideas.

ANTIPASTI

Make a platter of Parma or Black Forest ham and salami, a selection of cheeses such as goat cheese, soft cream cheese, feta, ricotta and/or mozzarella (look out for bocconcini), spreads such as hummus, tzatziki, tapenade or brinjal, marinated vegetables and fresh fruit, such as sweet melon, watermelon or nectarines. Serve with a selection of freshly baked breads, such as ciabatta, focaccia, sourdough bread and/or pitas. Also put plenty of olive oil, balsamic vinegar, sea salt flakes and black pepper on the table.

Marinated brinjals

Slice 2 brinjals or use whole baby brinjals. Brush with oil and season with salt and freshly ground black pepper. Bake the brinjals at 190 °C until done and golden brown. Mix 250 ml olive oil with 5 whole peeled cloves garlic. Transfer the brinjals into a bowl while still hot and pour over the olive oil. Leave to cool and store in the fridge.

Marinated mushrooms

Wipe 200 g button or portabellini mushrooms and put into a clean container. Blend 200 ml olive oil and 100 ml wine vinegar. Add 15 ml chopped garlic per mushroom, oregano, sugar, and 2 bay leaves and pour the dressing over the mushrooms. Leave overnight so the flavours can develop. Remove the bay leaves. The mushrooms will keep well in the fridge for several days.

Marinated feta cheese

Cube 3 rounds of feta cheese and drain. Put in a sterilised glass jar along with 2 chillies, sprigs of thyme, wide strips of lemon zest, and 2 cloves garlic. Fill the jar with olive oil, close it and marinate the cheese for about 4 hours.

Italian olives with tomatoes

Cut a cross in the bottom of each of 250 g black olives. Pour boiling water over 125 g sun-dried tomatoes to rehydrate them. Drain and pack the olives and tomatoes into a sterilised jar along with 2 cloves garlic, 1 fresh or dried chilli, and a sprig each of fresh thyme, rosemary and oregano. Blend 125 ml each olive oil and wine vinegar and pour on top to cover. Seal the jar and leave to stand at room temperature for 2 days.

Antipasti

BRUSCHETTA

Bruschetta is an open toasted sandwich made with Italian bread – perhaps that's where the idea of toasted cheese originated. Toast the bread slices over the coals and top with ingredients of your choice. Serve a platter of these toasted snacks before the main meal.

Basic bruschetta

Toast slices of bread on both sides until crisp (halve the slices if fairly big). Rub each slice with a peeled clove garlic if desired, drizzle with a little olive oil and sprinkle with salt. Serve as is or with a topping of your choice.

Ciabatta with caramelised tomato and Camembert

Toast slices of ciabatta and top each with rocket and a slice of Camembert and Black Forest ham. Top with a halved caramelised tomato.

Toasted rye bread with pesto and cheese

Toast rye bread slices and spread with feta, almond and paprika pesto (pg 14). Top with rocket and half a tomato.

VARIATION: Spread the toast with basil pesto and top with slices of mozzarella and rocket.

Toasted sourdough with nutty mushrooms

Fry 1 chopped onion, 1 chopped clove garlic and 60 ml chopped almonds in a little oil until fragrant. Stuff 4–6 brown mushrooms with the mixture. Dot with herb butter (pg 34) and bake at 200 °C until done. Serve on toasted sourdough.

Savoury bread bake

Spread slices of ciabatta or rye bread with a pesto of your choice. Arrange in a single layer in an ovenproof dish and scatter generously with mozzarella or feta cheese. Grill in the oven until the cheese has melted. Pile with rocket just before serving.

TARTLETS

Roll out ready-made puff pastry until slightly thinner. Cut the pastry into squares, rectangles or circles and top with any of the suggested toppings below, leaving the edges open. Lay the tartlets on a greased baking sheet and bake in a preheated oven at 200 °C until done and puffed.

Sun-dried tomato and feta topping

Chop 200 g sun-dried tomatoes and mix with 25 g pitted black olives, 180 ml onion marmalade (pg 14), and 70 g feta cheese. Spoon onto each pastry square and bake until done. *[pg 23, top]*

Tapenade and tomato topping

Spread olive tapenade over the pastry squares, crumble feta cheese over and top with a halved cherry tomato. Season to taste with salt, freshly ground black pepper and a pinch of sugar and bake until done.

Cream cheese and olive topping

Spread the pastry squares with a thick layer of herb cream cheese and press a pitted olive or sweet piquant pepper into the topping. Bake until done.

Salami and cheese topping

Scatter a little chopped salami in the middle of each pastry square and sprinkle with grated Cheddar cheese. Bake until done. *[pg 23, bottom]*

SNACKS

Spicy toasted nuts

Stir-fry 750 ml mixed nuts in 15 ml butter until golden brown. Mix 5 ml salt, 5 ml paprika, 3 ml mustard powder, 3 ml ground coriander, 2 ml ground nutmeg, and 1 ml cayenne pepper and sprinkle over the nuts. Mix and leave to cool.

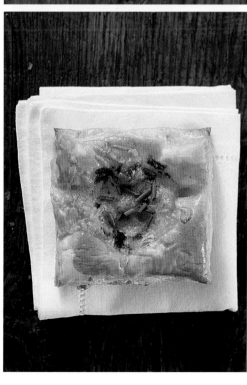

Cheese and tomato sticks

Thread bocconcini or mozzarella cheese cubes onto cocktail sticks along with cherry tomatoes and fresh basil if desired. Moisten with herb vinaigrette (pg 164) and leave to stand for at least 1 hour before serving.

Feta cheese and sweet melon sticks

Marinate cubes of feta cheese in a mixture of 3 ml toasted cumin seeds, 50 ml olive oil, the juice and zest of 1 lemon, and freshly ground black pepper to taste. Thread onto cocktail sticks along with pitted black olives and sweet melon balls.

'cattle are idolised on our farm and sent to auction reluctantly. If we had to choose our favourite type of meat, however, there's nothing that beats tucking into a tender piece of steak that has been prepared just right.'

succulent

Steaks

Most South Africans would agree: there are few things as satisfying as a tender steak.

Pleasing everyone takes some doing, though, because some swear rump steak is the ultimate

cut while others prefer sirloin or T-bone. Fortunately they all agree about one thing: fillet may

be the tenderest cut of all but isn't necessarily the most flavoursome.

Gone are the days steak was served with only a mushroom or monkey gland sauce and chips.

We've become more adventurous now and serve our steaks with a chocolate and chilli or brandy and

berry sauce. We stuff steaks with Camembert or avocado and serve them with beetroot or butternut

chips or garlic-and-feta mashed potatoes.

But there's a definite art to cooking a perfect steak and over the years braai fundis have discovered

all kinds of secrets to dishing up steaks at their most succulent best.

WHAT KIND OF STEAK TO BUY?

The most popular cuts are rump, T-bone, sirloin and fillet, all cut from the hindquarter of the animal and renowned for being tender and juicy. Fillet is the most tender of them all and the most expensive cut from the carcass.

Steaks can also be cut from certain parts of the forequarter and these are much cheaper than those cut from the hindquarter. Prime rib and club steaks, which are cut from the prime rib and wing rib respectively, can easily be used as substitutes for T-bone steak, while rib-eye steaks, cut from the prime rib, can be used instead of fillet, although the texture is much coarser.

BONELESS STEAK

FILLET STEAK
The whole fillet stretches from the loin to the rump along the spinal column and contains no bones or fat. Fillet slices are usually cut from the middle or loin section of the fillet and have a very fine texture.

SIRLOIN OR SCOTCH FILLET STEAK
These two kinds of steak are cut from the deboned rump. The sizes of these steaks vary, with Scotch fillet steaks being the bigger of the two. Scotch fillet steaks are sometimes also cut from the wing rib.

RUMP STEAK
These steaks are cut from the deboned rump and consist of a large layer of muscle with a fatty edge. Rump steaks are quite a bit bigger than sirloin steaks. A similar but smaller steak, the so-called 'ladies rump', is cut from the end of the rump.

STEAKS ON THE BONE

T-BONE AND PORTERHOUSE STEAK
You get the best of both worlds with T-bone and porterhouse steaks because they consist of a flavoursome piece of sirloin on one side of the bone and a tender piece of fillet on the other. T-bone steaks are cut from the section nearest the wing rib, while porterhouse steaks are cut from the section nearest the rump, which means they're quite a bit bigger than T-bones and a favourite with menfolk. They're easy to recognise by the T-shaped bone with a large eye muscle on the one side of the bone and a piece of fillet on the other. They contain no rib bones.

PRIME RIB STEAK
Prime rib steaks are cut from the forequarter of the carcass and are usually cheaper than T-bone steaks. Besides the spinal column (which is not T-shaped at this section) a prime rib steak also contains rib bones and a fatty edge on the opposite side to the rib bone. These steaks are larger than T-bone steaks and have a coarser texture.

CLUB STEAK
This delicious but oft forgotten little piece of steak is cut from the wing rib (in the hindquarter) and is therefore considerably cheaper than other steak cuts. It has an eye muscle and an even layer of fat and looks like half a T-bone or prime rib steak.

HOLLAND STEAK
Holland steak is easily recognisable thanks to the diamond pattern cut on the surface. It's cut from the topside and is delicious fried in butter in a pan until underdone.

TEXAS STEAK
This is a large steak that's also cut from the topside and contains part of the bone. Ensure the steak is from a younger animal and well matured before buying.

HOW TO COOK A PERFECT STEAK
The meat must be at room temperature, as this will ensure it cooks evenly. It will also be more tender. Score the fatty edges to prevent them curling during the cooking process.

The steaks must be at least 2.5–3 cm thick to ensure they are crisp on the outside and juicy and tender inside. If the steaks are cut too thin they can easily become dry and tasteless.

Cook the steaks as follows over the coals or in a pan: Ensure the braai grid or pan, preferably a griddle pan, is well heated. Brush the meat, not the pan, with oil. The coals must be glowing hot as the steaks must cook rapidly – the more robust they are the quicker they must be cooked so the outside is sealed and the juices are retained. Put the grid 5 cm above the coals and higher for thicker cuts such as porterhouse steak. Blow and fan the coals continuously to ensure they remain hot. Sear the steaks at least 1 minute on each side.

Don't turn the steaks until they are browned on the outside or they will stick to the pan or grid. Braai to the preferred degree of doneness (see guide, pg 27). Turn the meat using kitchen tongs and not a fork as the meat juices will be lost if the steaks are pricked.

Brush the meat with sunflower oil or melted butter from time to time to prevent it drying out over the hot coals. Leave the cooked steaks to rest for a few minutes to allow the meat juices to settle, but take care not to rest them too long. The rest of the meal must be ready so everyone can eat as soon as the meat is done.

HOW LONG SHOULD STEAKS BE COOKED?

Most people prefer their steaks medium-rare; overcooked steaks are taboo. The cooking time is always difficult to judge so here's a handy table:

BRAAI GUIDE FOR PORTIONS OF STEAK

Degree of doneness	Thickness of meat (cm)		
	2.5 cm	3 cm	4 cm
Rare	4–5 min.	5–6 min.	6–8 min.
Medium-rare	5–5½ min.	7–8 min.	8–9 min.
Medium	6–7 min.	8–10 min.	9–11 min.
Medium to well-done	7–8 min.	10–11 min.	11–12 min.

TOUCH TEST

You can also test the degree of doneness of the meat by touching it: a rare steak is very soft to the touch, a medium-rare steak will be slightly springy to the touch, a medium-done steak will be firmer to the touch and a well-done steak will not spring back at all.

VISUAL TEST

Rare: the outside of the steak is a greyish brown, the middle red and the rest pink.
Medium-rare: the middle of the steak is pink and it becomes greyer to the outside.
Medium-done: the middle is pink and gradually becomes greyish brown to the outside.
Medium to well-done: the meat is mostly greyish brown with a slightly pink tinge.
Well-done: the meat is greyish brown all the way through – not recommended for steaks.

HOW TO COOK A WHOLE CUT

Boneless beef cuts such as fillet, rump and sirloin can be braaied whole. Seal the outside of the meat well over very hot coals or in a hot pan. Raise the grid slightly so that the meat braais more slowly. Alternatively, roast in the oven at 160 °C.

COOKING TIMES FOR WHOLE CUTS

Rare: 15–20 minutes per 500 g meat plus 15 minutes extra (internal temperature 60 °C).
Medium done: 20–25 minutes per 500 g meat plus 20 minutes extra (internal temperature 65 °C).

Baste from time to time with the marinade, basting sauce, oil or butter or the meat will be dry. Wrap the cooked cut in aluminium foil and leave to rest in the warming drawer for about 10 minutes to allow the meat juices to settle.

TIP: Spread steaks lightly with Marmite before braaiing them.

TIP: Drizzle a little cooking oil over the fire as soon as you've put the steaks on the grid. The ensuing flames will sear the outside of the steaks, giving them a crisp outside layer.

GENERAL TIPS

How tender a steak is depends on several factors, such as the age and condition of the animal and how the meat was handled after the animal was slaughtered.

The tenderest cuts come from those parts of the animal that got the least exercise, such as the sirloin and rump. A rule of thumb is that the finer the texture of the meat the more tender it will be.

The meat must be well matured. Make a point of getting to know your butcher to ensure that you buy only the best meat. Alternatively, you can mature a smaller whole cut yourself by putting it on a wire rack over an oven pan and leaving it in the fridge, uncovered, for 4–5 days. It's pointless, however, trying to mature cut steaks this way – they will dry out.

HOW TO COOK THE PERFECT PEPPER STEAK

Pat dry 6 steaks of your choice with paper towel. Firmly but carefully press 45 ml coarsely ground black peppercorns onto both sides of the steaks using the palms of your hands. Braai the steaks as desired. Sprinkle with 60 ml hot brandy and ignite. Once the flames have died down scrape off the excess peppercorns, season the meat with salt and leave to rest briefly before serving.

STEAKS WITH TOPPINGS AND STUFFINGS

Whole cuts such as fillet and sirloin are ideal for stuffing. You can even stuff individual portions, such as sirloin steaks.

Witsand Kalahari fillet

Bertus van Niekerk, the tourism manager at the Witsand Nature Reserve in the Kalahari, treated me to this fillet. After the meat has been braaied, it's sliced and served in a coconut milk sauce with mealie meal dumplings.

MEALIE MEAL DUMPLINGS

4 x 250 ml mealie meal

5 x 250 ml water

10 ml salt

FILLET

1 whole beef fillet (1.5 kg)

100 ml olive oil

freshly ground black pepper
   to taste

1 green pepper, seeded and
   roughly chopped

1 red pepper, seeded and
   roughly chopped

1 yellow pepper, seeded and
   roughly chopped

1 bunch chives, roughly chopped

2 medium onions, roughly sliced

10 button mushrooms, roughly
   sliced

8 brown mushrooms, roughly sliced

4 fresh bay leaves

2 cans (410 g each) coconut milk

5 ml paprika

5 ml turmeric

salt to taste

2 fresh sprigs rosemary, chopped

12 cherry tomatoes

extra rosemary to garnish

DUMPLINGS: Prepare a stiff porridge with the mealie meal, water and salt. Cook until done. Roll the porridge into balls.

FILLET: Brush the fillet with a little of the olive oil, season with black pepper and leave to stand for 2 hours. Braai the fillet over hot coals until brown on the outside and still slightly pink in the middle. Wrap in aluminium foil and set aside. Heat 50 ml of the olive oil in a large pan over the coals. Fry the peppers, chives, onions, mushrooms and bay leaves until brown. Add the coconut milk, paprika and turmeric, reduce the heat and simmer for about 15 minutes. Season with salt to taste. Cut the fillet into thick slices and arrange in the pan along with the rosemary sprigs and mealie meal dumplings. Garnish with the tomatoes and fresh rosemary and serve immediately.

SERVES 6–8.

Wagon wheels fillet

This delicious fillet was one of the outstanding dishes served at the mealies-and-meat braai competitions held at Loskop Dam in the '90s.

STUFFING: Heat a little olive oil in a pan and stir-fry the vegetables until just soft but still crisp. Leave to cool and add the herbs and cheese. Season to taste.

FILLET: Halve the meat lengthways but do not cut all the way through. Butterfly the meat, flattening it slightly with the palm of your hand. Mix the mustard with a little olive oil and spread over the meat. Spoon the stuffing on the bottom half of the fillet and fold over the top half to close. Lightly season the meat with salt and pepper and arrange the bacon rashers on top, securing each with a kebab skewer inserted all the way through the fillet. Brown the fillet over very hot coals and then raise the grid higher above the coals. Braai to the preferred degree of doneness (see guide, pg 27). Mix the melted butter and lemon juice and baste the meat with the mixture while it's braaiing. Serve with champion mushroom sauce (pg 36).

SERVES 6–8.

1 whole beef fillet (1.5–2 kg)
± 60 ml wholegrain mustard
olive oil
salt and freshly ground black
   pepper to taste
1 packet (250 g) bacon rashers
50 ml melted butter
25 ml lemon juice

STUFFING
olive oil
1 onion, chopped
½ green pepper, seeded and
   chopped
3 cloves garlic, crushed
250 g portabellini mushrooms, sliced
250 ml roughly chopped vegetables
   such as baby marrows, carrots
   and baby corn
50 ml chopped fresh herbs such as
   chives, oregano and parsley
250 ml grated mozzarella cheese
salt and freshly ground black
   pepper to taste

Avocado beef fillet

This fillet was also one of the winning entries we tasted at a braai competition. Serve with the gooseberry salsa (below) or blue cheese sauce (pg 37).

Prepare the fillet as for the wagon wheels fillet above, but substitute the avocado for the stuffing and scatter with toasted almonds. (Do not spread the fillet with mustard if serving it with the gooseberry salsa.)

Gooseberry salsa

Blend all the ingredients together, cover and refrigerate to allow the flavours to develop. Serve with the avocado beef fillet.

SERVES 6.

STUFFING
1 avocado, cut into thick slices
salt and freshly ground black
   pepper to taste
toasted almonds

200 g fresh gooseberries, quartered
30 ml chopped fresh coriander
1 green chilli, seeded and chopped
5 spring onions, chopped
15 ml olive oil
10 ml white balsamic vinegar

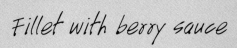
Fillet with berry sauce

Fillet with berry sauce

Slices of fillet served with a vibrant red sauce. Delicious!

SAUCE: Bring the sauce ingredients to the boil, stirring continuously until the sugar has dissolved. Simmer for about 5 minutes, or until slightly thickened and flavoursome.

FILLET: Season the fillet with salt and pepper, cover the outside with the mustard spread and braai until rare (pg 27). Cut the cooked fillet into thick slices, spoon the sauce over the top and serve. *[pg 30]*

SERVES 6–8

BERRY SAUCE

250 g frozen mixed berries

160 ml red wine vinegar

30 ml honey

45 ml brown sugar

dash of brandy

FILLET

1 whole fillet (1.5 kg)

salt and freshly ground black
  pepper to taste

mustard spread (pg 33)

Fillet with chocolate and chilli sauce

Chocolate with steak? Try it, it's sensational!

SAUCE: Bring the chilli, red wine and port to the boil and simmer until reduced by half. Add the stock and vinegar and whisk in the butter a bit at a time. Stir in the chocolate and season with salt and pepper.

FILLET: Season the meat with salt and pepper, brush with the oil and braai until rare (pg 27). Cut the cooked fillet into thick slices and spoon the sauce over each portion.

SERVES 4.

CHOCOLATE AND CHILLI SAUCE

1 red chilli, seeded and finely
  chopped

100 ml red wine

100 ml port

100 ml good meat stock

25 ml red wine vinegar

50 g butter

25 g dark chocolate, broken into
  squares

salt and freshly ground black
  pepper to taste

FILLET

750 g beef fillet

salt and freshly ground black
  pepper to taste

cooking oil

Fillet with feta cheese and spinach stuffing

STUFFING

125 g bacon rashers, chopped (optional)

1 onion, finely chopped

2 cloves garlic, crushed

± 150 g baby spinach or rocket leaves

125 g feta cheese, crumbled

FILLET

1 whole fillet (1.5 kg)

10–15 ml wholegrain mustard

salt and freshly ground black pepper to taste

25 ml olive oil

25 ml lemon juice

STUFFING: Fry the bacon, onion and garlic until the bacon is done. Add the spinach or rocket and heat until the leaves are just wilted. Add the feta cheese.

FILLET: Halve the meat lengthways, but do not cut all the way through. Butterfly the meat and flatten slightly with the palm of your hand. Mix the mustard, salt and pepper with a little of the olive oil and spread the meat with the mixture. Spoon the stuffing on the bottom half of the meat and fold over the top half to close. Lightly season the meat and secure the opening with kebab skewers. Mix the olive oil and lemon juice. Braai the fillet to the preferred degree of doneness (pg 27), basting from time to time with the oil and lemon juice mixture (or any basting sauce of your choice). Serve with nutty red wine sauce (pg 65) and char-grilled vegetables (pg 178).

SERVES 6–8

TIP: This stuffing goes well with sirloin steaks or even pork fillet.

Camembert sirloin steak

2 sirloin steaks (200 g each)

60 g Camembert cheese, sliced

mustard spread (pg 33)

25 ml melted butter

15 ml lemon juice or basting sauce of your choice

Cut a horizontal pocket in each steak and stuff it with slices of Camembert. Secure the pockets with cocktail sticks and brush the steaks with the mustard spread. Mix the butter and lemon juice. Braai the fillet to the desired degree of doneness (pg 27), basting from time to time with the butter and lemon juice mixture or other basting sauce. Serve with port sauce (pg 51), onion marmalade (pg 14) or cranberry sauce (pg 51). *[pg 38]*

SERVES 2

Rump steak with tomato and feta cheese

This rump steak is very popular at Le Must restaurant in Upington.

cherry tomatoes

whole cloves garlic, peeled

rosemary sprigs

brown sugar

olive oil

balsamic vinegar

rump steaks (200 g each)

mustard spread (pg 33)

1 thick slice feta cheese per steak

Preheat the oven to 200 °C. Put the tomatoes and garlic in an oven pan. Strip the leaves from the rosemary sprigs and scatter over the vegetables. Sprinkle liberally with brown sugar and drizzle with olive oil. Roast the tomatoes in the preheated oven until they are slightly caramelised. Sprinkle with a dash of balsamic vinegar. Cover the meat with the mustard spread and braai over the coals to the preferred degree of doneness (pg 27). Arrange the feta cheese slices on a baking sheet and grill until just browned on top. Arrange the steak on plates and top each steak with a slice of feta cheese and spoonful of tomatoes. Serve with potatoes.

EASY SPREADS, BASTING SAUCES AND MARINADES

Don't over prepare good meat – the idea is to allow the flavour of the meat to come through. You can't go wrong, however, using these simple spreads and marinades when cooking steak.

Mustard spread

Ideal for quickly spreading over a whole fillet before it goes on the braai.

Mix all the ingredients for the spread and cover the seasoned meat with the mixture. Braai the meat to the preferred degree of doneness (pg 27).

30 ml Dijon mustard
10 ml soy sauce
10 ml olive oil

Soy sauce marinade

This is YOU assistant food editor, Daleen van der Merwe's favourite marinade.

Mix all the marinade ingredients and pour over the meat. Turn the meat from time to time and marinate for at least 4 hours.

TIP: Pat the meat dry with paper towel after removing it from the marinade and before braaiing it.

TIP: Make a quick sauce to serve with the braaied meat by boiling the leftover marinade and adding a generous dash of balsamic vinegar.

250 ml soy sauce
250 ml olive or sunflower oil
60 ml lemon juice
4 cloves garlic, roughly chopped
2 red chillies, seeded and chopped
  (optional)

Blue cheese marinade

Di Doms of the Robertson valley was given the recipe for this marinade by Ina Paarman, who has inspired many a cook with her inventive dishes.

Mix all the marinade ingredients and marinate the meat for at least 3–4 hours. Bring the remaining marinade to the boil and serve as a sauce with the braaied meat.

SERVING SUGGESTION: Serve the steak with delicious mashed potatoes (pg 185).

TIP: For a quick marinade, mix 2 parts Worcestershire sauce and 1 part olive oil.

5 ml vegetable stock powder
125 ml blue cheese salad dressing
30 ml crumbled blue cheese
15 ml espresso coffee granules
30 ml boiling water
30 ml whisky

FLAVOURSOME BUTTERS

Steaks needn't be served only with a sauce. A pat of flavoured butter served on top of the braaied steak is just as delicious.

Herb butter on T-bone steak

A knob of butter is often all you need with a braaied steak.

125 g butter
10 ml chopped garlic
15 ml mustard powder
15 ml snipped chives
15 ml chopped fresh parsley
15 ml lemon juice
salt and freshly ground black
   pepper to taste

Heat 15 ml of the butter and sauté the garlic until soft. Cool slightly and mix with the remaining ingredients, including the rest of the butter. Spoon the butter mixture onto a sheet of clingfilm and shape it into a long roll 4–5 cm in diameter. Wrap it in the clingfilm and chill until hard and ice cold. Cut the butter into slices and put a slice on top of each braaied steak. *[pg 34–35]*

VARIATIONS – BLUE CHEESE BUTTER: Omit the mustard powder and stir 60 g crumbled blue cheese into the butter.

FETA CHEESE AND HERB BUTTER: Reduce the butter to 80 g, omit the mustard powder and stir in 100 g crumbled feta cheese.

Fillet steak with anchovy butter

Award-winning chef Reuben Riffel, of Reuben's in Franschhoek, likes serving braaied fillet steak with this anchovy butter and whole roasted vegetables.

Mix all the ingredients thoroughly. Shape into a roll, wrap in clingfilm and chill until hard. Top each braaied steak with a slice of anchovy butter.

125 ml anchovies in oil, excess oil
    drained, finely chopped
2 cloves garlic, chopped
60 ml lemon juice
60 ml chopped fresh parsley
freshly ground black pepper
    to taste
250 g soft butter

T-bone steak with herb butter and butternut chips

DELICIOUS SAUCES

Often the most memorable part of a steak meal is the sauce. Here's a selection of recipes for sauces you can serve with any one of your favourite cuts. See pg 50 for more sauces.

Champion mushroom sauce

Mushroom sauce is still a favourite with steak and it doesn't come much creamier, richer and more delicious than this. Especially good with T-bone steak.

25 ml butter
1 small onion, finely chopped
   (optional)
250 g button mushrooms, sliced
30 ml mushroom soup powder
300 ml fresh cream
salt to taste
few drops Tabasco sauce or freshly
   ground black pepper

Heat the butter in a saucepan over medium heat and brown the onion and mushrooms. Add the mushroom soup powder and sauté for 1 minute. Gradually stir in the cream and simmer while stirring continuously until the sauce has thickened. Add more cream if a thinner sauce is desired. Season with salt and Tabasco sauce or pepper.

SERVES 4.

VARIATION – MUSHROOM AND WINE SAUCE: Substitute 125 ml white wine and 125 ml vegetable stock for the cream.

Garlic sauce

1 onion, finely chopped
5 cloves garlic, crushed
cooking oil
125 ml fresh cream
125 ml milk
60 ml red wine
salt and freshly ground black
   pepper to taste

Sauté the onion and garlic in a little heated oil until soft. Add the cream, milk and wine, heat until the sauce comes to the boil and simmer until flavoursome and slightly thickened. Add seasoning to taste.

SERVES 4.

Mussel sauce

Serve this sauce with braaied fillet or sirloin steak.

250 ml fresh cream
1 can (85 g) smoked mussels,
   drained
10 ml instant white sauce powder

Bring the cream and mussels to the boil. Blend the white sauce powder with water to make a paste and stir into the cream mixture. Heat while stirring continuously until the sauce comes to the boil.

SERVES 4.

Chicken liver sauce

This sauce, another braai competition entry, is excellent with rump steak.

Sauté the chicken livers in the heated butter until brown on the outside and still slightly pink on the inside. Add the mushrooms and onion, followed by the stock and port and simmer until the sauce has reduced by half. Stir in the cream or yoghurt and parsley and season to taste. Do not bring back to the boil if you have used yoghurt. Serve each steak with a spoonful of the sauce.

SERVES 8.

500 g chicken livers
80 g butter
150 g button or portabellini
   mushrooms, sliced
1 onion, roughly chopped
200 ml vegetable stock
100 ml port
100 ml fresh cream or plain yoghurt
15 ml chopped fresh parsley
salt and freshly ground black
   pepper to taste

Classic green peppercorn sauce

A classic sauce, especially with steak on the bone.

Stir the butter, lemon juice and peppercorns over medium heat until the butter has melted. Remove from the heat and stir in the remaining ingredients. Return to low heat, whisking until the sauce has thickened slightly – do not allow it to come to the boil.

SERVES 4.

MOCK MUSTARD SAUCE: Mix a jar of prepared quality mustard with the same quantity cream. Heat without bringing to the boil. (See also easy mustard sauce on pg 68.)

90 g butter
40 ml lemon juice
60 ml green peppercorns in brine,
   drained
3 egg yolks
125 ml fresh cream
60 ml sour cream
20 ml Dijon or French mustard

Blue cheese sauce

Howick in KwaZulu-Natal is avocado country. Sandra Murphy of the Yellowwood Café likes to serve this piquant blue cheese sauce with steak and avocado.

Heat the butter and sauté the vegetables until transparent. Add the cheese and cream and, stirring continuously, simmer for about 2 minutes, or until creamy.

SERVES 4.

SERVING TIP: Braai any kind of steak to the preferred degree of doneness, arrange slices of avocado on the plate and serve with blue cheese sauce.

50 g butter
1 onion, finely chopped
1 leek, finely chopped
1 stalk celery, fincly chopped
5 ml finely chopped garlic
100 g blue cheese, crumbled
250 ml fresh cream

camembert sirloin steak with fried onion rings

SUPER SIDE DISHES

Most meat-lovers are happy to enjoy their juicy steak with only sauce on the side but serving it with any of these side dishes makes the meal that more special. Choose whichever dish you like – they go with any kind of steak.

Butternut or beetroot chips

These chips are excellent served with peri-peri mayonnaise or plain mayonnaise mixed with a pinch of peri-peri.

Heat the oil to 180 °C and fry the butternut (3–4 minutes) or beetroot (1 minute) chips until soft and lightly browned. Drain on paper towel. Just before serving, fry the chips again in very hot oil for 1–2 minutes, or until crisp. Drain on paper towel and sprinkle with coarse salt. *[pg 35]*

oil for deep-frying
1 kg butternut, peeled and cut into long strips or 4 medium beetroot, peeled and thinly sliced
coarse salt

SERVES 4.

Oven-baked butternut or brinjal

Slice butternut or brinjal into paper-thin slices. Place in a roasting pan and sprinkle with salt and oil. Bake in a preheated oven at 190 °C until cooked, crisp and golden brown.

Fried onion rings

The best-ever fried onion rings.

Cover the onion rings with iced water and leave in the fridge for 2 hours. Combine the self-raising flour and salt and gradually whisk in the cold water to make a smooth batter. Drain the onion rings and shake off the excess water. Put some cake flour in a plastic bag and shake the onion rings in the flour to coat completely. Heat the oil over medium-high heat. Dip the onion rings in the batter, one by one, and fry in the oil until brown. Drain on paper towel and season with salt or flavour enhancer. *[pg 38]*

4 onions, cut into 5 mm thick rings
500 ml self-raising flour
5 ml salt
250 ml cold water
cake flour
oil for deep-frying
salt or flavour enhancer (such as Aromat) to taste

SERVES 4–6.

'When our son brought his first buck home we knew exactly how to prepare and braai it in all kinds of delicious ways.'

mouthwatering Venison

I love the outdoors, especially the open plains of Namibia and the Kalahari. The windswept earth with its paucity of shade has its own singular beauty and lets you appreciate the small, simple things in life.

Here, among the red dunes, I've enjoyed the best-ever venison and it's here I was taught the secrets of preparing it to perfection by the experts, from venison sausage to *skilpadjies* (liver wrapped in caul fat).

BRAAI GUIDE AND TIPS

The same cooking times and tips for beef (pg 27) apply to venison.

TIP: There's no need to marinate venison in acidic vinegar sauces for days on end. Buttermilk (or use red wine to which a little buttermilk has been added) makes the perfect marinade. After all, when you have venison you want to taste the gaminess of the meat; it shouldn't taste like tamed beef.

Matumi venison fillet with cheese

At the Matumi Game Lodge near Hoedspruit in Limpopo the staff cater for large groups of visitors who can't wait to try the venison dishes.

4 pieces venison fillet (250 g each)
fresh lemon juice
bacon and mushroom sauce (pg 50)
salt and freshly ground black
   pepper to taste
4 slices Cheddar cheese

Marinate the venison fillets in a little lemon juice while preparing the sauce.

Braai the meat to the preferred degree of doneness (pg 27). Season with salt and pepper. Just before taking the fillets off the braai, top each with a slice of Cheddar cheese and heat until slightly melted. Serve with the sauce and potato chips or baked potatoes.

SERVES 4.

Venison fillet in caul

Game farms abound in the Karoo these days and each has a cook in the kitchen who's an expert when it comes to preparing meat, especially venison. Some of their best recipes were published in the book Camdeboo Karoo Venison. *This is one of them.*

1 venison fillet (such as gemsbok)
   (1.5 kg), membranes removed
soy sauce marinade (pg 33)
salt and freshly ground black
   pepper to taste
caul (available from your butcher),
   soaked in lukewarm vinegar
   water

Leave the meat to marinate in the soy sauce marinade for at least 12 hours, turning it regularly. Rub the meat with salt and pepper and wrap in the caul. Secure with kebab skewers and braai over coals (pg 27) for about 30 minutes – the meat must still be pink inside. Remove the skewers and slice the fillet. Serve with classic green peppercorn sauce (pg 37).

SERVES 6.

TIP: If caul is unobtainable, use rashers of bacon instead.

Stuffed venison back fillet

Blue cheese and venison are ideal companions. This fillet disappeared in a flash when YOU *assistant food editor, Daleen van der Merwe, treated the editorial team to a selection of venison dishes.*

Marinate the meat in the soy sauce marinade for at least 12 hours, turning it from time to time.

STUFFING: Heat the butter and sauté the chives, mushrooms and garlic until soft. Add the brandy and heat until all the liquid has evaporated. Remove from the heat and leave to cool. Stir in the blue cheese.

FILLET: Butterfly the marinated raw fillet, but do not cut all the way through. Season with salt and pepper and sprinkle with the gelatine. Spoon the stuffing on one half of the fillet, fold over the other half and season the meat with salt and pepper on the outside. Arrange the bacon rashers on top and secure them with kebab skewers. Braai over coals (pg 27) for about 30 minutes. Serve sliced with cranberry sauce (pg 51).

SERVES 6–8.

TIP: The gelatine helps to keep the meat intact when you carve it.

FILLET

1 venison back fillet (1.5 kg),
   membranes removed
soy sauce marinade (pg 33)
salt and freshly ground black
   pepper to taste
10 ml gelatine
300–500 g bacon rashers

STUFFING

50 g butter
2 chives, snipped
100 g button mushrooms, sliced
2 cloves garlic, crushed
60 ml brandy
200 g blue cheese, crumbled

Kalahari springbok loin

Elbé van der Merwe of Springbokvlei near Upington intersperses slices of deboned springbok loin with cheese and bacon, smothers the meat in cream and cooks it in aluminium foil.

Marinate the meat in the buttermilk marinade for about a day, turning it from time to time. Cut the marinated meat into 1 cm thick slices, but do not cut all the way through. Insert the bacon rashers between the slices, alternating them with the cheese slices. Pour over the cream and set aside for 2 hours. Season the meat with salt and pepper and wrap it in aluminium foil. Braai over cool coals for 20–30 minutes, or until the meat is brown on the outside and still slightly pink inside. Serve with easy green peppercorn sauce (pg 50).

SERVES 4.

TIP: Fairly small springbok or ostrich fillets can also be marinated in the buttermilk marinade and braaied.

1 whole springbok loin (600–800 g),
   deboned, membranes removed
buttermilk marinade (pg 48)
few rashers bacon, cut into
   smaller pieces
few thin slices Cheddar cheese
250 ml fresh cream
salt and freshly ground black
   pepper to taste

Deboned leg of springbok

While in the Colesberg region we were treated to a cruise on the Orange River in Anton du Plessis' boat, Lady Laatvy. As we cruised down the river he braaied us a leg of venison right there on the boat. Serve with griddlecakes (pg 151) and apricot jam.

1 leg of venison (such as springbok
    or reedbuck) (1.5–2 kg), deboned,
    membranes removed
pieces of lard or bacon
chopped fresh rosemary
salt

MARINADE
250 ml olive oil
250 ml lemon juice
30 ml flavour enhancer (such
    as Aromat)
5 ml chopped fresh rosemary
freshly ground black pepper
    to taste

Using a small, sharp knife make small incisions all over the leg. Sprinkle the lard with rosemary and stuff into the incisions.

MARINADE: Mix all the marinade ingredients and marinate the leg in the mixture for about a day.

Remove from the marinade and braai over coals (pg 27). Season with salt just before removing the meat from the fire.

SERVES 4–6.

TIP: The leg can also be marinated in herb marinade (pg 48).

Kalahari leg of springbok

In the early '90s we spent a week in the Kalahari near the Kgalagadi Transfrontier Park. Llewellyn and Mariaan Stadler of Askam are experts when it comes to venison and treated us to a wonderful selection of braaied meat.

250 g lard, thinly sliced
flavour enhancer (such as Aromat)
black pepper to taste
chopped fresh rosemary and
    parsley
1 leg of springbok (± 2 kg),
    well matured
red wine and buttermilk marinade
    (pg 48)
1 packet (250 g) shoulder bacon

Sprinkle the lard with flavour enhancer, black pepper, rosemary and parsley. Using a small, sharp knife make small incisions all over the leg and stuff with the lard. Place in the marinade for 4 hours. Arrange the bacon rashers on top of the leg, securing them with cocktail sticks. Wrap the leg tightly in aluminium foil and braai slowly for 1½–2 hours, or until just done but not dry. Remove the aluminium foil and braai until brown on the outside. Serve with quince or apple jelly. *[pg 45]*

SERVES 10–12.

Kalahari leg of springbok

Namibian stuffed venison loin

While on a visit to the south of Namibia we spent a few nights at Noachabeb near Grünau with Erich and Zelda von Shouroth in their old stone house, formerly a halfway house for German soldiers. One Sunday afternoon we had a braai with skilpadjies, *stuffed venison loin with sour sauce and venison sausage. What more could you want?*

1 venison loin (such as springbok,
    600–800 g, or gemsbok,
    1–1.2 kg), deboned
buttermilk marinade (pg 48)

STUFFING
bacon rashers, mushroom slices,
    grated Cheddar cheese and
    canned oysters or mussels
salt and freshly ground black
    pepper to taste

Marinate the venison in the buttermilk marinade for a day or two. Remove the meat from the marinade and halve lengthways, but do not cut all the way through.

STUFFING: Mix the stuffing ingredients and spoon on one half of the loin. Close, secure with string and season to taste with salt and pepper. Braai over cool coals for 20–30 minutes, or until golden brown and just done. Serve with sour sauce (pg 50). *[pg 46]*

SERVES 4–6.

Skilpadjies

If you're in the outdoors, such as on the Namibian plains, skilpadjies, *made with kudu liver wrapped in caul, are a delicious snack to serve while you wait for the rest of the meat to cook.*

Dice the liver and season with flavour enhancer, salt and pepper. Cut the caul into squares and spoon a little of the liver mixture onto each square. Fold to cover the liver mixture completely and secure with cocktail sticks. Braai slowly until golden brown and just cooked inside. Enjoy straight from the grill with sour sauce (pg 50).

TIP: Soak the liver in milk for about 1 hour to tone down the overpowering gamey taste.

kudu liver, cleaned and outer
    membrane and tubes removed
flavour enhancer (such as Aromat)
salt and freshly ground black
    pepper to taste
caul (available from your butcher)

Gosatie venison sausage

This recipe is from the Colesberg region, real sheep and game country. Elsabé Engelbrecht uses the sauce recipe from mutton sosaties to make this delicious venison sausage.

Cut the venison and pork or sheep's tails into cubes and add the salt and pepper. Mix the sauce ingredients and add to the sausage mixture. Mix well and marinate for 1–2 hours. Mince everything and add the lard, taking care not to overhandle the mixture. Attach a sausage nozzle to a meat mincer and stuff the casings with the meat mixture. Roll up the sausage, braai over medium coals until done and serve with griddlecakes (pg 151) and green fig preserve.

MAKES ± 20 KG RAW SAUSAGE.

TIP: The sosatie venison sausage freezes well.

SAUSAGE
10 kg venison (such as springbok)
2.5 kg fattish pork or sheep's tails
125–130 ml salt
25 ml freshly ground black pepper
10 kg lard or mutton fat, diced
500–700 g sausage casings, well
    cleaned

CURRY SAUCE
75–100 ml medium curry powder
25 ml flavour enhancer (such as
    Fondor)
375 ml chutney
75–125 ml brown vinegar
750 ml red wine

MARINADES

Any one of the following marinades can also be used for basting the meat while on the braai.

Herb marinade

This marinade is excellent with any meat, but is especially good with venison.

180 ml olive oil
180 ml cooking oil
60 ml lemon juice
5 ml freshly ground black pepper
125 ml chopped fresh parsley
15 ml chopped fresh oregano
3 bay leaves
1 large onion, chopped
4 cloves garlic, crushed

Mix all the ingredients and marinate the meat overnight.

MAKES ± 450 ML MARINADE.

Red wine and buttermilk marinade

I'm not fond of a venison marinade that has been made with red wine only.
But add a little buttermilk and it's a completely different story.

500 ml buttermilk
500 ml red wine
5 bay leaves
few pieces lemon zest
10 black peppercorns
few sprigs fresh rosemary or thyme

Mix all the ingredients and marinate the meat in the mixture overnight.

MAKES ± 1 LITRE MARINADE.

TIP: If you don't like red wine use white wine instead. You can also substitute half the buttermilk with cream.

Buttermilk marinade

Buttermilk ensures the meat is beautifully tender and is a great alternative if you don't like highly spiced or sweetish meat.

5 ml chopped fresh thyme
5 ml chopped fresh oregano
2 cloves garlic, crushed
250 ml buttermilk
30 ml lemon juice or the juice and
  zest of 2 lemons

Add the thyme and oregano to the garlic. Add the buttermilk and lemon juice, or the lemon juice and zest, and marinate the meat in the mixture overnight. Use the marinade to baste the meat while on the braai.

MAKES ± 250 ML MARINADE.

venison fillet with port sauce, blue cheese and figs

DELECTABLE SAUCES

These sauces go particularly well with venison, but see also pg 36 for other options.

Sour sauce

25 ml butter
2 eggs
150 ml sugar
1 ml salt
pinch pepper
150 ml white vinegar
125 ml mayonnaise

Soften the butter in a smallish pan. Add the eggs and whisk the butter and eggs with a fork until blended. Add the remaining ingredients, except the mayonnaise, and mix well. Heat slowly, stirring until thick and done. Remove from the heat and stir in the mayonnaise. Serve with venison or *skilpadjies* (pg 47).

MAKES ± 300 ML SAUCE.

Bacon and mushroom sauce

1 packet (250 g) bacon rashers,
    cut into pieces
½ onion, chopped
1 clove garlic, crushed
250 g brown mushrooms, sliced
500 ml fresh cream
5 ml beef stock powder
30 ml cornflour
50 ml water
3 ml soy sauce
1 ml paprika
salt and freshly ground black
    pepper to taste

Fry the bacon, onion, garlic and mushrooms in a pan until the bacon is just done. Add the cream and heat slowly, stirring continuously. Blend the stock powder and cornflour with the water to make a paste. Add to the cream mixture and bring to the boil, stirring continuously. Add the remaining ingredients.

MAKES ± 750 ML SAUCE.

Easy green peppercorn sauce

1 packet (65 g) white onion
    soup powder
10 ml cornflour
500 ml milk
250 ml fresh cream
30 ml green peppercorns in brine,
    drained

Mix the soup powder, cornflour and a little milk to a paste. Heat the remaining milk and cream, then add the paste and bring to the boil, stirring until thickened. Add the green peppercorns and heat through.

MAKES ± 750 ML SAUCE.

Cranberry sauce

Delicious with venison.

Bring all the ingredients, except the cornflour, water and yoghurt, to the boil, and simmer for about 10 minutes, or until fragrant. Thicken with cornflour blended with a little water. Remove the chillies and leave the sauce to cool slightly, then stir in the yoghurt.

MAKES ± 600 ML SAUCE.

500 ml water
10 ml grated fresh ginger (optional)
2 packets (100 g each) dried
   cranberries
30 ml brown sugar
2–3 whole red or green chillies
60 ml red wine vinegar or verjuice
30 ml wholegrain mustard
10 ml cornflour
water
30 ml plain yoghurt

Port sauce

This sauce is delicious with venison fillet, especially served with a slice of blue cheese and green fig preserve.

Heat all the ingredients, except the cream, in a saucepan and reduce by three-quarters. Stir in the cream. *[pg 49]*

MAKES ± 125 ML.

TIP: For a more robust sauce, substitute red wine for half the port.

250 ml chicken stock
125 ml port
5 ml balsamic vinegar
3 ml green peppercorns
25 ml fresh cream

Sweet Pinotage sauce

Bring the wine, honey, mustard and thyme to the boil and simmer until the mixture has reduced by half. Cool slightly, then stir in the yoghurt to add some creaminess.

MAKES ± 150 ML.

250 ml Pinotage
30–60 ml honey
15 ml wholegrain mustard
sprig of fresh thyme
15–30 ml plain yoghurt

POTJIEKOS

Kalahari gemsbok marrowbone potjie

1 kg venison marrowbones, cut into
   5 cm pieces
1 kg venison chops
1 large onion, sliced
few sprigs fresh rosemary and a
   few garlic chives
1 can (340 ml) beer
juice of ½ lemon
125 ml sherry
salt and freshly ground black
   pepper to taste
1 packet (500 g) prunes or mixed
   dried fruit, soaked
plain yoghurt

Brown the bones and chops in a large potjie over the coals. Add the onion and sauté until soft. Scatter the fresh herbs on top. Add the beer, lemon juice and sherry, cover and simmer until the meat is tender. Season with salt and pepper. Drain the dried fruit, add it to the potjie and simmer until plump. Stir in a little yoghurt just before serving. Scatter a little gremolata (see tip below) on top and serve with ash bread (pg 160) and jam. *[pg 52]*

SERVES 6.

TIP – GREMOLATA: Finely chop 2 cloves garlic and add about 60 ml chopped fresh parsley and the grated zest of 1 lemon. Scatter the gremolata over the meat just before serving.

Gemsbok have excellent marrowbones. If unobtainable use beef marrowbones. Mariaan Stadler of Askam serves ash bread with this potjie.

African venison potjie

Heat the oil in a large potjie over the coals and brown the meat all over. Remove the meat from the pot and fry the onions until soft. Return the meat to the pot and add the Worcestershire sauce, chutney, sherry or red wine, stock cubes and all the herbs and spices. Add enough water to cover all the ingredients and bring to the boil. Reduce the heat and simmer slowly for 1 hour until the meat is almost tender. Add the potatoes and cook until soft. Add the rest of the vegetables and cook until just done but still crisp. Serve with *krummelpap*.

SERVES 4–6.

50 ml cooking oil

500 g kudu loin, cut into
   3 cm cubes

500 g springbok loin, cut into
   3 cm cubes

2 onions, roughly chopped

30 ml Worcestershire sauce

45 ml chutney

250 ml sherry or red wine

2 beef stock cubes

4 bay leaves

5 ml leaf masala

10 ml mixed dried herbs

3 ml ground coriander

5 ml ground cumin

water

4 potatoes, peeled and cut
   into pieces

250 g button mushrooms,
   wiped clean

1 red pepper, seeded and
   cut into large pieces

1 green pepper, seeded and
   cut into large pieces

5 baby marrows, cut into
   large chunks

At Mama Africa, a restaurant in Long Street, Cape Town, this fragrant venison potjie is served with krummelpap.

'Pork is my favourite meat. I'm so fond of it that when we have a braai at home a pork chop is always put on the fire, just for me. My children prefer pork spare ribs and love to devour them straight from the grill.'

versatile *Pork*

Pork meat is light and, because the fat is on the outside, you can decide whether you want to indulge or not. I must confess I sometimes can't resist sampling the crisp crackling, but I mostly restrain myself and stick to only the deliciously tender meat. The secret when cooking pork (like all other meat) is never to overcook it.

GENERAL BRAAI TIPS

Pork is always tender but ensure you only buy your meat from a reputable butcher and select meat from a young animal. Pork that is slaughtered at the municipal abattoir is completely safe and doesn't need to be cooked to death.

Pork chops must, however, be well done so the meat is no longer pink inside, although it should still be juicy, tender and packed with flavour.

Test for doneness by pricking the chops with a meat skewer – if the juices run clear the chops are done. Take care not to overcook the chops or they will be dry and tasteless.

The following cuts are suitable for braaiing: spareribs (cut from the rib ends of the breast), loin (whole or cut into chops), fillet, ribs (cut from the rib), chump, thick rib and leg (especially suitable for kebabs) and neck, which can be cooked whole or in slices. The chops must not be cut too thin or they will dry out – 2 cm is the ideal thickness.

Season a large cut well before putting it on the braai and rub the fatty rind with salt so it can crisp nicely.

Marinades and basting sauces go well with pork and help to keep the meat succulent.

Braai a whole loin or spareribs for about 1 hour. Cut it into chops and continue braaiing until just done.

Pork is best cooked over a medium to cool fire; lower the grid towards the end of the braai time.

BRAAI GUIDE

Cut	Size	Cooking time	Internal temperature
Rib, loin, shoulder and neck chops	2 cm thick	12–14 min.	71 °C
Whole loin	1.5–2.25 kg	1¾ hr	71 °C
Spareribs	1.5–1.75 kg	1–1½ hr	71 °C
Loin steaks	350–450 g	25–35 min.	71 °C

CHOPS

Mustard pork chops

Mustard and pork is a classic winning combination. A little sweetness also improves the flavour of the meat.

Season the chops on both sides with salt, pepper and cumin. Mix the mustard and brown sugar and set aside. Braai the chops over medium coals until done, brushing one side of each chop with the mustard mixture a few minutes before the end of the braai time. Braai until the mixture begins to bubble. Do not turn. Serve immediately with sweet melon salad (pg 171). *[pg 59]*

SERVES 6–8.

6–8 pork chops, thickly cut and
    fatty edges removed
salt and freshly ground black
    pepper to taste
1 ml ground cumin
30 ml wholegrain mustard
30 ml brown sugar

Sweet 'n sour pork chops

Blend all the sauce ingredients and brush the meat with the mixture while braaiing over medium coals. Take care the chops don't burn – the coals must not be too hot.

SERVES 4–6.

4–6 pork chops

LEMON AND HONEY SAUCE
60 ml lemon juice
60 ml honey
60 ml soy sauce
2 cloves garlic, finely chopped
5 ml finely grated fresh ginger
    (optional)
15 ml finely chopped fresh
    coriander (optional)

Sweet 'n sour pork is an old favourite and the characteristic flavour couldn't be easier to achieve. Simply mix equal quantities of lemon juice, honey and soy sauce and brush over the pork chops or whole cuts, and even over chicken.

Orange and mustard pork steaks

For me, pork is at its tastiest best simply cooked and drizzled with a little sauce. This sauce is delicious with whole cuts, steak, chops and, my favourite, pork neck.

6 pork steaks, cut from the
  deboned neck, loin or leg

ORANGE AND MUSTARD SAUCE
250 ml orange juice
30 ml apricot jam
20 ml Dijon or wholegrain mustard
7 ml bruised fresh ginger (optional)
15 ml soy sauce
30 ml butter

Heat all the sauce ingredients and boil rapidly for 5 minutes.

Braai the steaks over medium coals, brushing with the basting sauce from time to time.

SERVES 4–6.

Spiced pork chops

4–6 pork loin chops or 1 whole rib

SPICE MIXTURE
7 ml coarse salt
7 ml paprika
15 ml mustard powder
15 ml dried oregano or thyme
15 ml ground coriander (optional)
2 ml cayenne pepper (optional)
5–7 ml ground cumin (optional)
2 ml ground cinnamon (optional)
olive oil

Mix all the spice ingredients you have chosen with olive oil to make a paste and rub the meat with the mixture. Leave to stand for about 30 minutes before braaiing over medium coals.

SERVES 4–6.

TIP: Mix the dry spice ingredients and store in an airtight container. Mix with olive oil just before using.

VARIATION: Add 1–2 chopped cloves garlic and 15 ml grated lemon zest.

BASIC MARINADE FOR PORK: 2 parts olive oil, 1 part fresh lemon juice, 30 ml soy sauce, 30 ml chutney and 5 ml braai spice.

You can use only basic seasonings such as salt, paprika and mustard or give the chops an African twist with spices such as coriander, cumin and cinnamon.

Mustard pork chops with sweet melon salad

Stuffed pork chops

Pork chops are a long-standing favourite and are even better when stuffed.

CHEESE STUFFING

250 ml fresh white breadcrumbs

125 ml grated cheese such as
  mozzarella, Parmesan or blue
  cheese

mayonnaise

5 ml coriander or sun-dried tomato
  pesto (optional)

CHOPS

4–6 pork chops, thickly cut

60 ml olive oil

30 ml lemon juice

15 ml Dijon mustard

STUFFING: Mix the breadcrumbs with the cheese. Add enough mayonnaise to mix to a thick paste. Add the coriander or tomato pesto, if using.

CHOPS: Make a horizontal incision in each pork chop to make a pocket, taking care not to cut all the way through. Fill the pockets with the stuffing and secure with cocktail sticks. Blend the olive oil, lemon juice and Dijon mustard and set aside. Braai the chops over medium coals until done, basting with the oil mixture from time to time. Serve with champion mushroom sauce (pg 36) and quick chickpea salad (variation 1, pg 172). *[pg 60]*

VARIATION: You can also use the vegetable stuffing for the wagon wheels fillet (pg 29).

SERVES 4–6.

Smoked pork chops

Mustard is an ideal companion to pork, especially if the meat is smoked. Add sweetish fruit such as pineapple and you have a winning combination. Because the pork chops are smoked they need just a few minutes on the fire.

Mix all the rub ingredients and rub the chops with the mixture. Leave to stand for about 1 hour. Braai the chops for 3–4 minutes a side, or until done. Season with salt and serve with pineapple and mustard sauce or quick fruity sauce.

SERVES 6–8.

8 smoked pork chops
salt

RUB
2 ml curry powder
2 ml cayenne pepper
2 ml ground cinnamon
5 cardamom pods, seeds removed
  and bruised (optional)
7 ml Dijon mustard
7 ml apple cider vinegar
15 ml oil

Pineapple and mustard sauce

This sauce is also excellent with cold cuts.

Whisk the eggs and add the remaining ingredients. Bring to the boil over very low heat, stirring continuously. Serve with smoked pork chops.

2 extra-large eggs
250 ml pineapple juice
50 ml white wine vinegar
125 ml brown sugar
15 ml cake flour
20 ml mustard powder
2 ml turmeric
1 ml salt

Quick fruity sauce

Mix all the sauce ingredients and serve with smoked pork chops.

1 banana, mashed
1 small can crushed pineapple
60–100 ml sweet chilli sauce
few drops lemon juice

SPARERIBS

While searching the YOU *files for recipes I came across no less than 20 recipes for spareribs alone, which just goes to show how popular this finger-licking good cut is.*

Spareribs with rooibos marinade

This basic marinade made with tomato sauce, chutney and mustard will appeal to most. You can also use pork belly cut into strips instead of spareribs.

1.5 kg spareribs, cut into 3 sections
7 ml salt
freshly ground black pepper
    to taste

MARINADE
250 ml strong rooibos
125 ml sunflower oil
125 ml tomato sauce
125 ml chutney
30 ml Worcestershire sauce
60 ml grape vinegar or
    30 ml balsamic vinegar
5 ml crushed garlic
5 ml mustard powder
1 onion, finely chopped
10 ml grated fresh ginger or
    5 ml ground ginger
30 ml brown sugar

Mix all the marinade ingredients and bring to the boil. Simmer for 15 minutes or until fragrant. Cool completely.

Put the spareribs in a non-metallic dish and pour over the marinade. Marinate for at least 4 hours. Remove the meat from the marinade, pat dry and season with salt and pepper. Braai over medium to cool coals for 45–60 minutes until tender and done. Turn the ribs regularly, brushing with the marinade from time to time. Cut the ribs into pieces and brush with more marinade. Set the grid close to the coals and braai the ribs rapidly on all sides until crisp. Bring the leftover marinade to the boil and serve with the spareribs, along with lemon slices.

SERVES 4–6.

TIP: Add extra flavour by rubbing the spareribs with a spice mixture (pg 58) instead of only salt and pepper. The optional ingredients give the meat a wonderfully spicy flavour. Leave to stand for about 30 minutes and baste with the marinade while braaiing.

Apple sauce

Spareribs served with this sauce appear regularly on the menu in Reuben Riffel's award-winning restaurant, Reuben's, in Franschhoek.

4 Granny Smith apples, peeled,
    cored and chopped
60 ml sugar
125 ml water
60 ml butter
30 ml Szechuan or black pepper

Heat the apples, sugar and water, and simmer until the apples are soft. Add the butter and blend in a food processor until smooth. Season with pepper and serve with pork.

Eastern spareribs

The flavours of the East are made for pork – soy sauce and honey especially are a winning combination. These spareribs disappeared in no time when we prepared them in the test kitchen.

Mix all the marinade ingredients and marinate the meat for at least 3–4 hours. Remove the meat from the marinade, pat dry and season with salt and pepper. Braai the ribs over medium to cool coals for 45–60 minutes, or until tender and done. Turn the ribs regularly and brush with the marinade from time to time. Cut the ribs into portions and brush with more marinade. Set the grid lower over the fire and braai the ribs until crisp. Bring the leftover marinade to the boil and serve with the ribs, along with lemon slices. *[pg 63]*

SERVES 4–6.

TIP: You can also use this marinade for deboned whole pork loin, neck or leg of pork.

1.5 kg spareribs, cut into 3 sections
salt and freshly ground black
   pepper to taste

MARINADE
80 ml honey
60 ml soy sauce
45 ml oyster sauce (optional)
15 ml sesame oil
30 ml soft brown sugar
7 cm piece fresh ginger, grated
3 cloves garlic, crushed
2 red chillies, seeded and chopped,
   or 1 ml cayenne pepper (optional)
juice of 2 limes or lemons
grated zest of 1 orange
1 ml ground cinnamon and/or
   cumin
1 ml five-spice powder (optional)

Pork neck with fillet and blue cheese stuffing

WHOLE CUTS

You can never go wrong with pork; it's the one kind of meat that is always tender. It's not fatty either as most of the fat is on the outside and can be cut off if desired.

Pork neck with fillet and blue cheese stuffing

Tender deboned pork neck, whole or cut into chops, is my favourite. Our butcher, Alan Allsop, is renowned for his pork neck stuffed with beef fillet. I've added extra flavour with blue cheese, nuts and herbs. Alternatively, you can stuff the neck with only the fillet or blue cheese, always a winner with pork.

Fold open the deboned pork neck and make a shallow incision in the middle, making sure that the ends are still intact. Season the pork neck and beef fillet and sprinkle with lemon juice. Make small incisions all over the pork neck and beef fillet and insert the garlic strips. Evenly scatter the stuffing ingredients over the inside surface of the pork neck and place the beef fillet on top. Fold up and secure with string. Season to taste on the outside. Mix all the topping ingredients and spread the meat with the mixture. Braai the neck over medium coals for 1½–2 hours. Cover with a dome lid or aluminium foil. Alternatively, cook the neck in a kettle braai. Brush with a little olive oil from time to time to prevent the meat drying out. Serve with a nutty red wine or apple sauce (pg 62) and delicious mashed potatoes (pg 185). *[pg 64]*

SERVES 6.

TIP: Pork is cooked when it is no longer pink on the inside and the meat juices run clear.

MEAT
½ pork neck, deboned and rind removed
1 fairly small beef fillet
salt and freshly ground black pepper to taste
lemon juice
4–6 cloves garlic, thinly sliced

STUFFING
250 ml fresh white breadcrumbs
60 ml chopped walnuts
30 ml chopped fresh sage
30 ml chopped fresh thyme
60 ml crumbled blue cheese

TOPPING
30 ml Dijon mustard
10 ml soy sauce
10 ml olive oil

Nutty red wine sauce

I first tasted this delicious sauce with stuffed pork fillet on the guest farm Fraai Uitzicht near Robertson. It's also excellent with pork neck with fillet and blue cheese stuffing (above).

Heat the wine along with the onion and rosemary until reduced by half. Strain the liquid. Blend the cornflour with the fruit juice and add to the sauce. Stirring continuously, simmer the sauce until it thickens. Add the nuts and season with salt, pepper and sugar. Remove from heat and stir in the yoghurt.

400 ml red wine
1 onion, chopped
2 sprigs fresh rosemary
20 ml cornflour
125 ml pear and apple juice
50 g chopped walnuts
salt, freshly ground black pepper and sugar to taste
15 ml plain yoghurt

Mediterranean pork loin

Versatile pork is not only delicious with Eastern flavours, it also goes well with Mediterranean flavours such as rosemary, garlic and parsley. But in this dish it's the smoked paprika that adds the special touch.

1 pork loin (± 1.25 kg), deboned
   and cut into 3 equal pieces

SMOKED PAPRIKA
AND HERB TOPPING
4 cloves garlic, chopped
60 ml olive oil
30 ml chopped fresh parsley
15 ml chopped fresh oregano
15 ml chopped fresh rosemary
5 ml chopped fresh thyme
10–15 ml smoked paprika
salt and freshly ground black
   pepper to taste

Blend all the topping ingredients in a food processor to make a thick paste. Spread all over the pork loin, put the meat on a plate, cover with clingfilm and leave in the fridge for at least 4 hours, preferably overnight. Remove the meat from the fridge and let it come back to room temperature. Braai over medium coals for 30–35 minutes, basting with extra olive oil from time to time. Cover with a dome lid or aluminium foil. Alternatively, cook the meat in a kettle braai. *[pg 67]*

SERVES 6.

TIP: The topping mixture can be made more than a week in advance and can be kept in the fridge until needed.

Italian leg of pork

The Italians know how to cook a leg of pork. This leg is best served with roasted peppers (pg 180).

1 leg of pork (1.5 kg), deboned
coarse salt
fresh rosemary sprigs
8 cloves garlic, sliced
freshly ground black pepper
   to taste
15 ml dried oregano
4 dried bay leaves, crushed
30 ml honey
30 ml olive oil
30 ml lemon juice

ANCHOVY SAUCE
2 anchovy fillets, mashed
30 ml capers, finely chopped
5 ml prepared mustard
10 ml white wine or balsamic vinegar
2 cloves garlic, crushed
90 ml chopped fresh herbs such as
   parsley, chives and rosemary
100 ml olive oil

Butterfly the leg of pork so it lies flat. Make diagonal incisions in the rind. Put the meat in a colander, rind side up, and pour over boiling water. Pat dry. Rub the rind well with coarse salt and stuff the incisions with rosemary and garlic slices. Scatter the black pepper, oregano and bay leaves on top and drizzle the leg with honey. Set the grid close to hot coals and braai the leg, rind side down, until the rind begins to brown. Turn over. Set the grid higher and remove some of the coals. Braai over medium to cool coals for 1½–2 hours, or until done. Cover with a dome lid or aluminium foil while braaiing. Alternatively, cook the meat in a kettle braai. Brush the leg with the combined olive oil and lemon juice from time to time to prevent the meat from drying out. Serve with anchovy sauce.

ANCHOVY SAUCE: Blend all the sauce ingredients, except the olive oil. Add the olive oil a little at a time while stirring continuously. Serve with the Italian leg of pork.

SERVES 8–10.

TIP: The anchovy sauce is also good with roast leg of lamb.

Mediterranean pork loin

Smoked leg of pork

1 whole smoked leg of pork
5 ml mustard powder
3 black peppercorns
2 fresh or dried bay leaves
2 stalks celery
2 carrots

GLAZE
125 ml smooth apricot jam
15 ml mustard powder

Put the leg of pork into a large saucepan or potjie and add the remaining ingredients, except those for the glaze. Cover with cold water, put the lid on and cook until tender. Remove the leg from the liquid. Remove the rind and set it aside (see tip). Cut a diamond pattern in the fat layer. Blend the apricot jam and mustard powder and spread over the surface of the leg. Braai over hot coals until golden brown all over. Brush with the glaze mixture from time to time. Serve with easy mustard sauce (below). *[pg 69]*

SERVES 8.

VARIATION: Use ginger preserve instead of the apricot jam. Chop the ginger pieces finely and add a generous quantity of the syrup.

Easy mustard sauce

45–60 ml wholegrain mustard
60 ml olive oil
300 ml mayonnaise
300 ml plain yoghurt
15 ml sugar
salt and freshly ground black
   pepper to taste

Put the mustard in a shallow bowl. Slowly add the olive oil, mixing well. Add the mayonnaise and yoghurt and mix well. Season with sugar, salt and pepper and serve with the pork.

TIP: Cut the rind into long strips and fry on one side of the grid until crisp. Serve the crackling as a pre-dinner snack.

If you're planning to serve smoked leg of pork and don't have an oven on hand, try cooking it over the fire.

'Leg of lamb was reserved for Sunday lunch,
even now when more than 20 of us get
together as a family on Sundays.'

melt-in-the-mouth

Lamb

On Bergendal, our family farm at the top of Piekenierskloof near Citrusdal, we also farmed sheep.

Come the April holidays — there were no December holidays for us because that's harvest time on

a fruit farm — the chops and sausage were carefully treated and packed, enough for the suppertime

braais. Around the braai fire the quality of the meat was always discussed, and then a Bergendal chop

always came out tops. When we're in Langebaan we often cook a leg of lamb over the fire. Leftovers

are thinly sliced and marinated in a sauce with exotic Eastern flavours — delicious on bread with a

salad for lunch the next day.

GENERAL TIPS

The most popular lamb cuts for braaiing are those from the rib and loin (whole or cut into chops), leg (whole, deboned or cut into chops), shoulder, and thick rib or chump, which produces the best chops.

Chops must be cut fairly thick, about 2–2.5 cm is perfect. Thinner chops dry out over the coals. Score the fatty edges and season the chops before putting them on the braai.

Lamb improves if left a few days to mature: choose large cuts (not chops; they will dry out) with a generous layer of fat, wipe the meat with a cloth soaked in vinegar and leave in the fridge, uncovered, for 2–5 days to mature.

Lamb is juiciest and most tender when still pink inside (medium done) and is much more flavoursome than well-done lamb. Braai over medium coals.

Meat cut	Size	Cooking time
Loin, rib or chump chops	2.5 cm thick	10–12 min.
	5 cm thick	14–16 min.
Leg of lamb steaks	2.5 cm thick	10–12 min.
Leg of lamb, deboned and butterflied	1.7 kg	55–60 min.
Leg of lamb, deboned and rolled	1.7 kg–2.7 kg	1½–2 hr
Ribs, whole	1.2 kg–1.5 kg	1¼–1½ hr

The internal temperature of these cuts should be 71 °C for medium done.

Turn braaied chops into something really special by topping them with blue cheese, my favourite, or feta cheese when they're just about done.

Lamb chops with cheese topping

CHOPS

Mediterranean lamb chops

Lamb chops taste best when not overseasoned. But you can't go wrong basting the meat with a basic olive oil and lemon juice marinade flavoured with garlic and fresh herbs such as rosemary and/or thyme while they're on the braai.

Mix all the marinade ingredients. Arrange the chops in a stainless steel dish and pour over the marinade. Marinate for 30 minutes to 3 hours.

Insert long rosemary sprigs in the thick part of each chop and braai over medium coals to the preferred degree of doneness. Baste with the remaining marinade from time to time and season with salt and pepper. Serve with roasted vegetables and skewered potato wedges (pg 182).

SERVES 4.

VARIATION – STUFFED LAMB CHOPS: Cut a pocket in the thick part of rib chops and fill with one of the stuffings for leg of lamb (pg 81–85). Secure the openings with cocktail sticks and braai the chops to the preferred degree of doneness.

TIP: Tie sprigs of herbs such as rosemary and thyme in a bunch and use as a brush to apply the marinade. Alternatively, scatter the herb sprigs on the coals so the aromatic flavours can penetrate the meat.

TIP: Thread 3–4 chops onto a kebab skewer by inserting the skewer through the thickest part of the meat. Ensure the fatty edges of all the chops point in the same direction. Arrange the meat on the grid, fatty sides down, and braai until the fat is crisp. Remove the skewers and braai the chops flat sides facing down.

4 lamb chops
rosemary sprigs
salt and freshly ground black
    pepper to taste

MARINADE
45 ml white wine (optional)
60 ml olive oil
15 ml lemon juice or white
    wine vinegar
20 ml sun-dried tomato pesto
    (optional)
3–5 cloves garlic, finely chopped
30–45 ml chopped fresh herbs
    such as oregano, thyme,
    rosemary and parsley
5 ml grated lemon zest

Lamb chops with cheese topping

Season the chops to taste and brush with olive oil. Braai over medium coals until nearly done. Meanwhile mix the remaining ingredients. Arrange the cooked chops on a baking tray and spoon a little of the mixture on top of each. Grill rapidly under the oven grill until the topping is lightly browned and bubbling. *[pg 72]*

SERVES 4.

VARIATION: Substitute feta cheese for the blue cheese.

TIP: You can return the chops to the fire and heat them until the topping just begins to bubble. Do not turn the chops.

6 lamb chops
salt and freshly ground black
    pepper to taste
olive oil
100 ml fresh brown breadcrumbs
1 small onion, finely chopped
    (optional)
5 ml finely chopped fresh rosemary
    or thyme
125 ml crumbled blue cheese
50 ml mayonnaise

Butterflied leg of lamb

WHOLE LEG OF LAMB AND SHOULDER

HOW TO COOK WHOLE LAMB CUTS OVER THE COALS

Brush the grid and the meat with oil. Brown and seal the cut on both sides over hot coals. Brush well with the marinade or basting mixture, set the grid higher and braai over medium coals. Try to keep the temperature constant by adding extra coals or lowering the grid as needed. Turn the meat frequently and baste constantly with the marinade. Cover with a lid or a thick layer of aluminium foil while the meat is braaiing. A whole 1.7 kg deboned leg should be cooked after 50–60 minutes (about 30 minutes longer for stuffed leg or leg with bone). Leg of lamb can be served still slightly pink on the inside. Leave the meat to rest for about 10 minutes before carving it.

TIP: Whole cuts are easiest to cook turning them slowly on a spit over the coals until crisp and brown and meltingly tender. They are just as good cooked in a kettle braai until juicy and brown.

Butterflied leg of lamb

The easiest way to cook a whole leg of lamb over the coals is to debone and butterfly it. This delicious leg of lamb is special enough for Christmas lunch. Marinate it the day before and start braaiing it early in the morning. Take care you don't overcook it though – it should still be slightly pink but not glassy on the inside. The leg can stand in the sauce until you're ready to serve lunch. Carve it into very thin slices.

MARINADE: Mix all the marinade ingredients and rub the mixture into the meat. Put the meat in a stainless steel dish and marinate in the fridge overnight.

Braai the leg over medium coals for about 50 minutes or until juicy and tender and still slightly pink inside. Baste with the remaining marinade from time to time and season with salt and pepper. You can also cover the leg with a dome lid or thick layer of aluminium foil while braaiing it. Serve with chickpea and butternut salad (pg 172). *[pg 74]*

SERVES 6.

TIP: Use the buttermilk marinade on pg 48 and leave the meat to marinate in the mixture overnight.

HINT: The easiest way to marinate leg of lamb is to leave it in bought salad dressing overnight. Braai over the coals to the desired degree of doneness.

1 leg of lamb (1.7–2 kg), deboned
    and butterflied
salt and freshly ground black
    pepper to taste

MARINADE
250 ml tomato sauce
250 ml olive oil
60 ml soft brown sugar
30 ml apple cider vinegar
25 ml grated fresh ginger
4 cloves garlic, crushed
50 ml soy sauce
leaves of 3 sprigs of rosemary

Greek leg of lamb

1 leg of lamb (± 1.7 kg), deboned
    and butterflied if desired
salt and freshly ground black
    pepper to taste
2 cloves garlic, cut into strips
sprigs of fresh rosemary or thyme
375 ml orange juice
juice and zest of 1 lemon
125 ml dry white wine
125 ml olive oil

Season the leg of lamb with salt and black pepper and make small incisions all over the surface of the meat. Insert the strips of garlic and most of the rosemary or thyme sprigs into the incisions. Mix the orange juice, lemon juice and zest, wine and olive oil and pour over the leg of lamb. Scatter more rosemary or thyme sprigs on top. Marinate for at least 3 hours.

Braai the leg over medium coals for 50–60 minutes, basting with the remaining marinade from time to time. Carve thinly and serve as described below. *[pg 77]*

SERVES 6.

Greeks like to serve their meat lukewarm. This leg of lamb is especially good sliced and serve in pita breads with pickles, feta cheese and olives.

Greek lamb pot

To make this deliciously creamy dish you need ouzo, the potent aniseed-flavoured spirit from Greece. It's the ideal way to serve leftover lamb – the cooked slices of lamb are stewed in a mouthwateringly good creamy sauce.

20 ml butter
1 clove garlic, crushed
20 ml tomato paste
50 ml ouzo
250 ml fresh cream
1 can (400 g) artichokes, drained
750 g sliced leftover leg of lamb
    (see Greek leg of lamb above)

Heat the butter and garlic in a potjie and stir in the tomato paste, ouzo and cream. Mix well. Add the artichokes and meat slices as soon as the cream turns pink and simmer until heated through. Serve with rice or potatoes.

SERVES 4.

Greek leg of lamb

I was lucky enough to grow up in a large family and we often headed into the mountains over weekends for a braai. Recently we returned to our favourite spot on the flat rock with its view over the farm. In the north you can see the fog rolling in from the sea and to the south you can just make out the outline of Table Mountain. We feasted on roasts and stuffed pork neck, roasted vegetables, salads and homemade bread washed down with wine from the boutique cellar on the farm.

Turkish shoulder of lamb

Years ago when Pamela Schippel was still at Pick 'n Pay's cookery school she treated us to a magnificent Middle Eastern braai. Perhaps that's where I became hooked on spicy food.

1 shoulder or leg of lamb (1.5 kg),
　　deboned
125 g butter

MARINADE
75 ml olive oil
25 ml dried oregano
1 onion, finely grated
4 cloves garlic, crushed
20 ml ground cumin
3 ml freshly ground black pepper
juice of 1 lemon

MARINADE: Mix all the marinade ingredients. Put the meat in a stainless steel dish and pour over the marinade so the meat is completely coated. Marinate for 12 hours in the fridge.

Braai the meat over medium coals to the desired degree of doneness. Baste with the marinade from time to time. Heat the butter until brown, taking care not to burn it. Carve the meat into slices and pour over the browned butter. Serve with Turkish pita breads, plain yoghurt mixed with a little chopped cucumber and flavoured with cumin, and a mixed salad.

SERVES 4.

Creamy spiced lamb

This flavoursome dish made with leftover braaied meat is a meal on its own. Use as a filling for pita breads.

15 ml olive oil
1 onion, thinly sliced
2 cloves garlic, crushed
5 ml grated fresh ginger
10 ml ground cumin
10 ml ground coriander
5 ml paprika
10 ml dried chilli flakes
500 g leftover leg of lamb, cut into
　　fairly thick strips
180 ml plain yoghurt
chopped fresh coriander

Heat the olive oil in a pan and stir-fry the onion, garlic, ginger, spices and chilli flakes until fragrant. Add the meat and stir to coat. Add a little water if necessary. Stir in the yoghurt and heat slowly until warm, but do not bring to the boil as the liquid will split. Stir in the coriander. Cut open hot pita breads and fill with fresh leaves, such as rocket, baby spinach and endive, and the spicy meat mixture. Scatter diced cucumber, tomato and onion on top.

SERVES 4.

STUFFED LAMB CUTS

Use shoulder of lamb as an alternative to leg of lamb; it's more affordable and just as tasty.

Mediterranean lamb roll

In Greece lamb stuffed with spinach and cheese and cooked over the fire is a favourite. This dish is much simpler and is stuffed with feta cheese flavoured with plenty of garlic. You can baste the meat with olive oil and lemon juice while braaiing it or experiment with buttermilk marinade (pg 48).

Butterfly the meat to make it easier to roll up. With the meaty side facing up, season with salt, pepper and half the lemon juice and zest. Mix the feta cheese with half the garlic and spoon the mixture down the middle of the meat. Roll up firmly, securing with string at regular intervals. Rub the outside of the meat with coarse salt, pepper and olive oil, sprinkle with the remaining lemon juice, lemon zest and garlic and braai over medium coals for 1½–2 hours, or until done. Baste with olive oil from time to time. Leave the meat to rest for 10 minutes before carving. Serve with hot pita breads, a Greek salad and tzatziki.

SERVES 6–8.

VARIATION: Substitute ricotta for the feta cheese and, for a creamier stuffing, mix it with a little quality mayonnaise and basil or sun-dried tomato pesto.

VARIATION: Add 12 pitted and chopped green olives or a few piquant peppers or green peppercorns to the stuffing.

1 leg or shoulder of lamb (± 1.5 kg), deboned
salt and freshly ground black pepper to taste
juice and zest of 1 lemon
400 g feta cheese with black pepper
5 cloves garlic, finely chopped
coarse salt
olive oil

Mexican leg of lamb

Mexican leg of lamb

The leg of lamb is marinated in a spicy marinade before it's put on the braai. The marinade is not as hot as you would expect, so if you like your food hot, add some chillies. Carve the meat into slices and roll up in tortillas along with a generous scoop of guacamole and/or Texas beans (below).

MARINADE: Mix all the marinade ingredients. Put the leg of lamb in a stainless steel dish and pour over the marinade. Leave to marinate in the fridge overnight.

Braai the leg of lamb over medium coals until done (pg 72). Baste with the marinade from time to time. Season with salt and pepper. Leave the leg to rest for 5–10 minutes before carving. Serve in tortillas as described above. *[pg 82]*

SERVES 6.

1 leg of lamb (1.6 kg), deboned
   and butterflied
salt and freshly ground black
   pepper to taste

MARINADE
15 ml grated fresh ginger
30 ml chopped fresh coriander
15 ml curry powder
10 ml ground cumin
30 ml hot chutney
4 cloves garlic, crushed
15 ml tomato paste
45 ml butter, melted
350 ml plain yoghurt
pinch cayenne pepper

Texas beans

Heat a little olive oil in a pan and fry the onions and garlic with the spices until soft. Add the red pepper and stir-fry for 1 minute longer. Season with salt and pepper and add both cans of beans. Heat until warmed through and scatter coriander leaves on top. Serve with braaied lamb chops and a spoonful of guacamole or with Mexican leg of lamb. Roll up in tortillas if preferred.

SERVES 4.

olive oil
2 onions, chopped
3 cloves garlic, crushed
5 ml ground cumin
5 ml ground coriander
1 red pepper, seeded and chopped
salt and freshly ground black
   pepper to taste
1 can (410 g) red kidney beans,
   drained
1 can (410 g) butter beans, drained
chopped fresh coriander

Guacamole

Mix together 3 ripe avocados (peeled, stones removed, and roughly chopped), 30 ml lemon juice, 1 chopped tomato, 1 small chopped red onion, 1–2 seeded and chopped fresh chillies, 15 ml chopped fresh coriander, 2 crushed cloves garlic, 30 ml sour cream, and salt and freshly ground black pepper to taste. Chill until needed. Serve with the Mexican leg of lamb.

Mutton rib roll with dried fruit filling

Marchel van Niekerk treated us to this stuffed mutton rib cooked over the fire when we visited Witsand in the Kalahari. You can also roast the roll in the oven and just brown it over the coals.

1 mutton rib, deboned
50 ml white vinegar
15 ml coriander seeds
½ packet (250 g) mixed dried fruit
1 litre boiling water
1 packet (250 g) bacon, diced
2 onions, chopped
125 ml fresh breadcrumbs
15 ml finely chopped fresh
    rosemary
30 ml finely chopped fresh parsley
5 ml salt
freshly ground black pepper
250 ml dry white wine

Remove all the excess fat from the rib. Rub the meat with the vinegar and coriander seeds and leave to stand for 2 hours. Soak the dried fruit in the boiling water for 30 minutes, drain and cut into small pieces using scissors. Fry the bacon over medium heat until crisp and golden brown and drain on paper towel. Fry the onions until brown and return the bacon to the pan. Add the dried fruit, breadcrumbs, herbs, salt, pepper and white wine and simmer until the mixture has thickened slightly. Remove from the heat and leave to cool. Unroll the deboned rib, spoon the stuffing lengthways down the middle and roll the meat up tightly. Secure with string at regular intervals. Braai the rib over hot coals until sealed all over. Raise the grid, cover the rib with aluminium foil and braai for about 1½ hours, or until tender and done. Turn from time to time. Serve with baked sweet potatoes (variation 4, pg 179). *[pg 84]*

SERVES 8.

Royal leg of lamb

MARINADE: Mix all the marinade ingredients. Put the leg in a stainless steel dish, pour over the marinade and marinate overnight in the fridge.

STUFFING: Heat a little olive oil in a pan and sauté the onions and garlic until soft. Add the spices and stir-fry gently. Remove from the heat and stir in the lemon zest, dates and nuts. Remove the meat from the marinade and season all over to taste. Spoon the filling on the meaty side of the leg, roll it up carefully and secure with string. Braai over medium coals for about 1½ hours, basting with the leftover marinade from time to time. Serve with fried onion rings and couscous flavoured with chopped fresh coriander.

SERVES 8.

TIP: Substitute 6–8 dried figs or apricots for the dates. Soak the fruit in sherry or rooibos before using.

Dates and figs have been served at royal courts for centuries. Here they are used to make a stuffing flavoured with spices. This is a dish fit for a king.

1 leg of lamb (1.5–1.8 kg), deboned and butterflied
salt and freshly ground black pepper to taste

MARINADE
juice and zest of 2 oranges
30 ml honey
2 ml ground cumin
125 ml sherry or sweet wine

STUFFING
olive oil
2 small onions, chopped
3 cloves garlic, crushed
2 ml turmeric
5 ml ground cinnamon
10 ml ground cumin
finely grated zest of 2 lemons
12–16 pitted dates, finely chopped
50 g pecan nuts, chopped

Moroccan leg of lamb

STUFFING: Add the boiling water to the couscous and leave to stand until the water has been absorbed. Fluff with a fork. Toast the pine nuts and almond flakes in a dry pan until lightly browned. Remove from the pan. Heat the oil and fry the onion, garlic and spices until fragrant. Mix the toasted pine nuts, almond flakes, onion mixture, fresh herbs and raisins with the couscous. Proceed as for the royal leg of lamb (above).

SERVES 8.

1 leg of lamb (1.5–1.8 kg), deboned and butterflied
salt and freshly ground pepper

STUFFING
250 ml boiling water
80 ml couscous
125 ml pine nuts
125 ml almond flakes
45 ml olive or cooking oil
1 large onion, chopped
2 cloves garlic, crushed
7 ml ground coriander
7 ml ground cumin
5 ml ground cinnamon
10 ml chopped fresh mint
60 ml chopped fresh coriander
80 ml seedless raisins

quick and easy

Skewers, burgers and boerewors

You don't have to turn a braai into a major production with loads of meat. It's also fun making a fire for just a piece of boerewors or home-made burgers. Alternatively, have a braai with skewered treats for a change — they also add variety to the usual steak-and-chops-type braai.

SKEWERED FOOD

Food served on a skewer, be it meat or vegetables, never fails to impress. It also provides variety and the food goes much further as you can combine more expensive treats with affordable ingredients. When it comes to skewered food it's the marinade or basting sauce that provides most of the flavour so don't skimp in this area. Supermarkets also stock a selection of ready-made marinades, but preferably choose those that don't contain additives such as MSG, colorants and preservatives.

Best sosaties

There are loads of sosatie recipes. This is a traditional one made with milk (you can also use buttermilk) to tenderise the meat.

MARINADE

30 ml cooking oil

2–3 large onions, sliced

3 cloves garlic, crushed

30 ml medium curry powder

5 ml turmeric

2 ml ground coriander

½ red chilli, seeded and chopped,
    or 1 ml cayenne pepper

3 bay leaves

15 ml grated fresh ginger or
    5 ml ground ginger

45–60 ml apricot jam

350 ml wine vinegar

500 ml milk

MEAT

1.5 kg deboned lamb or mutton,
    cut into 25 mm cubes

1.5 kg deboned pork, cut into
    25 mm cubes

50 dried apricots

1 packet (250 g) bacon rashers,
    cut into pieces (optional)

MARINADE: Heat the oil in a saucepan and sauté the onions and garlic until soft. Add the curry and stir-fry for 2 minutes more. Add the remaining marinade ingredients, except the milk. Simmer for 10 minutes, remove from the heat and leave to cool before adding the milk.

MEAT: Put the meat in a non-metallic dish, pour over the marinade and leave to marinate in the mixture for at least 24 hours. Thread the meat cubes onto skewers, alternating them with the apricots and bacon. Braai over medium coals until done, brushing with the marinade from time to time.

SERVES 10–12.

VARIATION – YOGHURT MARINADE: Mix 250 ml plain yoghurt, 2 grated onions, 4 crushed cloves garlic, juice of 2 lemons, 10 ml paprika and 10 ml ground cumin.

Jenny's pork kebabs

Jenny Morris, of Giggling Gourmet fame, prefers to use only pork when making kebabs. She uses pork neck, my favourite cut because it's always tender.

MARINADE: Mix all the marinade ingredients.

Put the meat in a non-metallic dish, pour over the marinade and leave to marinate for at least 5 hours. Thread the meat onto kebab skewers and braai over medium coals until just done, taking care not to overcook the meat or it will be dry. Serve with coleslaw.

SERVES 4–6.

1 kg pork neck, cubed

MARINADE
250 ml plain yoghurt or buttermilk
15 ml ground coriander
15 ml turmeric
5 ml ground cumin
3 cloves garlic, crushed
3 cm piece fresh ginger, grated
30 ml chopped fresh coriander
1 large chilli, seeded and finely
   chopped
10 ml finely grated lemon zest
5 ml salt

Venison kebabs

Put the meat in a non-metallic dish and marinate overnight in the buttermilk, to which the garlic has been added. Thread the meat cubes onto the rosemary sprigs, alternating them with the peppers, onion and apricots. Braai the kebabs over medium coals, brushing with olive oil from time to time until done.

SERVES 8.

1 kg kudu fillet, cut into 3 cm cubes
100 ml buttermilk
5 cloves fresh garlic, peeled
8 sprigs of rosemary (± 20 cm long),
   all the leaves stripped except for
   a small tuft at the top
1 green pepper, seeded and cut
   into large squares
1 red pepper, seeded and cut into
   large squares
1 onion, cut into wedges
16 dried apricots
olive oil

At Tini Neethling's game and guest lodge, Langberg, near Kimberley, venison is in big demand among the guests. These sosaties are always a winner.

Curried chicken kebabs

At Jemima's in Oudtshoorn these kebabs are served with mango achar salsa, which is ridiculously easy to make.

1 kg deboned chicken breasts,
    skin on, cubed

CURRY PASTE
50 ml mild curry powder
5 ml masala (optional)
1 ml turmeric
30 ml olive oil
salt
juice of 1 lemon

CURRY PASTE: Mix all the curry paste ingredients.

Mix the chicken cubes with the curry paste, ensuring they are well coated. Thread the chicken cubes onto kebab skewers and braai over medium coals until done. Serve with mango achar.

MAKES 10–12 KEBABS.

Mango achar salsa

1 jar (410 g) mango achar
1 can (400 g) coconut milk
fresh coriander leaves
toasted desiccated coconut
unsalted peanuts

Pour off the excess oil from the mango achar and purée the achar in a food processor. Add the coconut milk and stir well. Garnish with coriander, coconut and peanuts.

Dukkah chicken skewers

Melissa van Hoogstraten, of Melissa's deli fame, serves these chicken skewers with basil mayonnaise as a starter.

500 g chicken fillets, skinned,
    deboned and sliced into strips
2 eggs
250 ml cake flour
20 ml chicken or meat rub
2 cans (100 g each) Egyptian
    dukkah
oil for deep-frying

Thread the chicken strips onto long bamboo skewers. Whisk the eggs in a bowl. Mix the flour and meat rub in another bowl and put the dukkah in a third bowl. Dip the chicken strips into the flour mixture, then into the egg and finally into the dukkah. Deep-fry for 5–10 minutes in heated oil, or until just done. *[pg 91]*

SERVES 4.

Basil mayonnaise

330 ml good quality mayonnaise
200 ml basil pesto

Blend the mayonnaise and pesto, spoon into a bowl and serve with the dukkah chicken skewers. *[pg 91]*

Dukkah chicken skewers

Chicken or pork satay

Strips of chicken or pork are threaded onto skewers and served with satay sauce (peanut sauce) from the East.

500 g deboned chicken or pork,
   cut into strips
sesame seeds (optional)

MARINADE
30 ml olive oil
30 ml soy sauce
5 ml soft brown sugar
1 clove garlic, crushed
1 onion, finely chopped
grated lemon zest
10 ml ground coriander
10 ml ground cumin
5 ml turmeric

MARINADE: Blend all the marinade ingredients.

Put the meat in a non-metallic dish, pour over the marinade and leave to marinate for 2–4 hours in the fridge, but preferably overnight. Thread the meat strips onto skewers and braai over medium coals until done. Sprinkle with sesame seeds if desired and serve with satay sauce and Thai achar (pg 93). *[pg 92]*

SERVES 4–6.

Satay sauce (peanut sauce)

Heat the oil and fry the garlic until soft. Add the curry paste and stir-fry slightly. Add the remaining ingredients, except the lemon juice, reduce the heat and simmer until the sauce has reduced and thickened slightly. Flavour with lemon juice.

15 ml olive oil

1 clove garlic, crushed

15–30 ml curry paste

15 ml brown sugar

125 g unsalted peanuts, finely chopped

1 can (400 g) coconut milk

a little lemon juice to taste

Thai achar

Mix all the ingredients and serve with chicken or pork satay.

60 ml white sugar

50 ml white vinegar

2 ml salt

1 small onion, chopped

¼ English cucumber, diced

2 red chillies, seeded and finely chopped

Espetadas

Espetadas are so popular they appear on the menus of just about every Portuguese restaurant. These oversize kebabs are threaded onto a special metal skewer complete with stand and a small dripping bowl for catching the juices. On the island of Madeira, the meat cubes were originally threaded onto a fresh bay twig, brushed with olive oil, sprinkled with garlic and coarse salt and braaied. Venison prepared this way is also delicious.

MARINADE: Mix all the marinade ingredients.

Put the meat in a shallow, non-metallic dish, pour over the marinade and marinate for 6 hours to 2 days in the fridge. Remove the meat cubes and thread onto 6–8 long skewers. Heat the marinade for 2–3 minutes and lightly brush the meat with the mixture. Keep the remaining marinade warm. Put the grid 15 cm above hot coals and braai the espetadas: 7 minutes for rare and 9–10 minutes for medium done. Turn the espetadas regularly, brushing with the marinade from time to time. Serve with roast potatoes or chips and a salad.

SERVES 6.

1.5 kg beef rump or fillet, or venison loin or fillet, cut into 4 cm cubes

MARINADE

200 ml olive oil

50 ml lemon juice

25 ml wine vinegar

25–50 ml ground coriander (optional)

4 cloves garlic, finely sliced

4 fresh bay leaves, torn

10 ml salt

20 ml freshly ground black pepper

Chicken espetadas

These espetadas are a cross with South African sosaties because the meat is cut into big cubes, as for espetadas, and then threaded onto skewers along with apricots and onions, as for sosaties. Brush the espetadas with the apricot basting sauce while on the braai.

APRICOT BASTING SAUCE

125 g dried apricots

500 ml apricot juice

1 onion, finely chopped

2 cloves garlic, crushed

30 ml curry powder

50 ml sunflower oil

2 bay leaves

juice of ½ lemon

salt and freshly ground black
 pepper to taste

MEAT

± 1.2 kg chicken or turkey breast,
 deboned and cut into 4 cm cubes

salt and freshly ground black
 pepper to taste

onions (preferably red onions),
 cut into large chunks

soft Turkish apricots

lemon or fresh bay leaves

red pepper, seeded and cut into
 large chunks

BASTING SAUCE: Put the apricots and juice in a saucepan, cover and simmer for 30 minutes, or until soft. Put in a food processor and blend. Fry the onion, garlic and curry powder in the heated oil until fragrant. Add the remaining ingredients, including the puréed apricots, simmer for 10 minutes and then leave to cool.

MEAT: Season the meat with salt and pepper, and then place in the basting sauce, cover and leave to marinate in the mixture for at least 2 hours. Thread the meat onto large kebab skewers, alternating with the onions, apricots, leaves and pepper cubes. Braai the meat 20 cm above hot coals for 30–40 minutes, basting regularly with the apricot sauce.

SERVES 6.

Kofta

This Turkish speciality is basically a large meatball shaped around a skewer and cooked over the coals.

500 g lean mince (lamb or beef)

2 eggs

300 ml fresh breadcrumbs

2 small onions, finely grated

2 cloves garlic, crushed

30 ml each chopped fresh parsley
 and/or mint

5 ml each ground cumin and turmeric

2 ml ground cinnamon

2 ml chilli powder

salt to taste

Mix all the ingredients well. Press a handful (60 ml) of the mixture onto the end of a skewer. Braai over medium coals for about 7 minutes a side or until cooked through. Serve with hummus (pg 95) and crushed wheat or Mediterranean couscous salad (pg 174).

SERVES 6.

VARIATION: Wrap a rasher of bacon around mini-meatballs and thread them onto skewers.

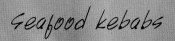

Seafood kebabs

Hummus

Drain 2 cans chickpeas (410 g each) well and purée in a food processor. Add 1 crushed clove garlic, 60 ml tahini (sesame seed paste), 60 ml lemon juice, 125 ml plain yoghurt and 60 ml water. Blend well.

Kebabs

Thread chicken, pork or fish cubes onto skewers, alternating the cubes with vegetables of your choice. Leave to marinate in one of the following marinades for at least 1 hour.

Soy and honey marinade

- 25 ml chilli or sesame oil
- 1 clove garlic, crushed
- 45 ml soy sauce
- 20 ml sweet chilli sauce
- 20 ml sun-dried tomato pesto
- 5 ml honey
- 15 ml chopped fresh coriander
- 15 ml chopped fresh parsley
- ½ packet (50 g) unsalted peanuts, toasted and finely chopped (optional)

Mix all the marinade ingredients. Make kebabs of your choice, put them in a non-metallic dish, pour over the marinade and leave to marinate in the mixture, preferably overnight. Braai over hot coals until just done.

MAKES 100 ML.

TIP: Use vegetables such as mushrooms, baby onions, sweet peppers and/or cooked butternut cubes.

Thai marinade

- 2 red chillies, seeded and finely chopped
- 1 clove garlic, crushed
- 15 ml castor sugar
- 15 ml lime juice
- 45 ml fish sauce
- 15 ml rice wine vinegar
- 45 ml water
- 60 ml olive oil
- 30 ml white wine vinegar
- 5 ml grated fresh ginger
- 10 ml finely chopped lemon grass
- 15 ml chopped fresh coriander
- 60 ml coconut milk or plain yoghurt (optional)

Mix the chillies, garlic, sugar, lime juice, fish sauce, rice wine vinegar and water, stirring until the sugar has dissolved. Add the remaining ingredients. Make fish, chicken or pork kebabs of your choice, put them in a non-metallic dish, pour over the marinade and leave the kebabs in the fridge to marinate in the mixture for several hours but preferably overnight. Braai the kebabs over hot coals until just done.

MAKES 160 ML.

SERVING SUGGESTION: Remove the meat from the skewers and serve with flat breads such as tortillas, shredded vegetables, and a dollop of hummus (pg 95) or coriander pesto (pg 14). Serve with fresh lime quarters.

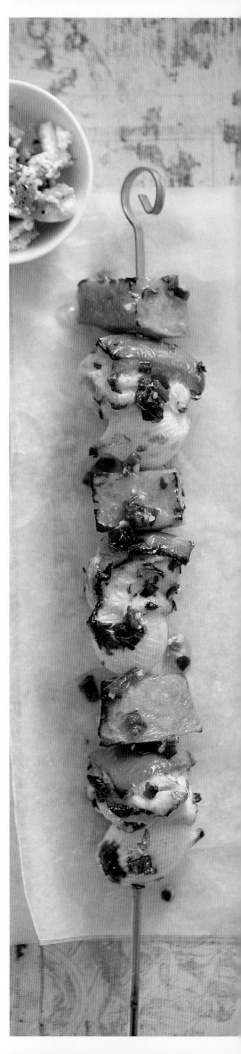

Seafood kebabs

Put a raw prawn inside a calamari tube and thread onto a kebab skewer or lemon grass stem. Marinate in one of the marinades (pg 96). Thread a small tomato onto each skewer and braai over medium coals for ± 2 minutes a side, or until done. Brush with the remaining marinade and season with salt and freshly ground black pepper before serving. *[pg 95]*

Pork kebabs

Thread pork cubes, red and yellow pepper wedges and halved baby brinjals onto kebab skewers. Pour over soy and honey marinade (pg 96) and braai over medium coals until done. Serve with cucumber or avocado salsa (below). *[pg 97]*

Chicken kebabs

Thread chicken or pork cubes, pickling onions and butternut and red pepper cubes onto kebab skewers and leave to marinate in Thai marinade (pg 96). Braai over medium coals until done and tender. Serve with cucumber or avocado salsa. *[pg 96]*

Cucumber salsa

2 nectarines or 1 papino, diced	salt
¼ English cucumber, diced	3 ml sugar
1 cm piece fresh ginger, grated	10 ml rice wine vinegar
1 small red chilli, seeded and chopped	chopped fresh coriander

Mix all the ingredients and serve with chicken or pork kebabs.

Avocado salsa

1 large or 2 small avocados, peeled	1 small chilli, seeded and chopped
3–4 rounds feta cheese, crumbled	salt and freshly ground black pepper
2–3 spring onions, chopped	to taste
juice of ½ lemon	

Mix all the ingredients and serve with chicken or pork kebabs.

BURGERS

Burgers are a great alternative to chops for a braai. Provide a selection of breads and fillings so guests can assemble their own burgers. Make home-made burgers – they're much nicer than the ready-made ones.

Gourmet burgers

Basic burger patties

1 onion, finely chopped
1 large clove garlic, crushed
cooking or olive oil
1 kg lean beef mince
30 ml chopped fresh parsley
1 egg, lightly whisked
salt and freshly ground black
  pepper to taste

Sauté the onion and garlic in a little oil until soft. Leave to cool and add the remaining ingredients. Mix gently, taking care not to overmix or the burgers will be tough. Shape the mixture into 10 burger patties, flattening them slightly with the palm of your hand. Chill until needed and cook over medium-hot coals until brown on the outside but still juicy and slightly pink inside. *[pg 98]*

MAKES 10 BURGERS.

VARIATION 1 – ECONO-BURGERS: Add 250 ml fresh white or brown breadcrumbs to the basic burger mixture to make it go a bit further.

VARIATION 2 – CHEESE BURGERS: Add 250 ml grated Cheddar cheese, 30 ml prepared mustard and 5 ml paprika to the basic burger mixture.

VARIATION 3 – SPICY BURGERS: Add 5 ml ground cumin, 5 ml ground coriander, 3 ml nutmeg, 25 ml chopped fresh coriander and the zest of 1 lemon to the basic burger mixture.

TIP: Like steak, burgers must be crisp and brown on the outside, juicy inside and packed with natural flavour throughout.

Bread

Ordinary burger rolls are fine but also try using Portuguese bread rolls, ciabatta, focaccia, pitas and even griddlecakes for a change. Toast over the coals before using.

Burger extras

- A selection of fresh lettuce leaves such as butter lettuce, rocket, mizuna or endive, tomato, and a cucumber salsa.
- Slices of cheese, including Camembert or Brie, with onion marmalade (pg 14) or caramelised onion rings (pg 160) or a topping of crumbled feta or blue cheese.
- Slices of tomatoes, brown mushrooms and pineapple lightly browned over the coals.
- Strips of roasted red and yellow peppers, skin removed.
- Fried bacon and egg.
- Caramelised onion rings (sprinkle with sugar and a little balsamic vinegar while frying).
- A little mayonnaise, chutney, prepared mustard or tomato sauce to spread on the bread before topping with the burger.
- Basil or sun-dried tomato pesto to spread on the bread before topping with the burger.
- A mixture of pesto and mayonnaise to spoon on top of the burger.
- Mashed avocado mixed with cottage cheese to spoon on top of the burger.
- Grated cucumber mixed with plain yoghurt to spoon on top of the burger.
- Cucumber ribbons to pile on top of the burger.

Chicken burgers

Chicken breasts also make delicious burgers. Flatten deboned chicken breasts with the palm of your hand and sprinkle liberally with soy sauce. Add 5 ml Chinese five-spice powder or ground cumin to cake flour and roll the chicken breasts in the mixture. Heat a little oil in a large pan over the coals and fry the chicken breasts until just done. Take care not to overcook the chicken breasts or they will be dry.

SAUCE: Mix 30 ml sweet chilli sauce and 45 ml coconut milk. Put a fried chicken breast on each toasted bread roll and spoon a little of the sauce on top. Using a vegetable peeler cut an English cucumber into long strips and stack on top of the chicken. Garnish with bean sprouts.

VARIATION: Use deboned hake fillets instead of chicken.

SAUSAGE

No braai is complete without sausage. Boerewors is the best option, because then at least you know the sausage consists of 90 per cent meat. Instead of enjoying boerewors on its own, try one of these delicious serving suggestions.

Gourmet boerewors rolls

VARIATION 1: Arrange a selection of lettuce leaves on a hotdog or other roll and put a piece of boerewors on top. Spoon a little braised onion (below) and a few cherry tomato halves moistened with mustard vinaigrette (pg 164) on top. *[pg 101]*

BRAISED ONION: Slice 2 onions into rings and fry in a mixture of olive oil and butter until soft. Season with salt, freshly ground black pepper and a little sugar. Add 5 ml Dijon mustard, 30 ml balsamic vinegar and 15 ml honey. Simmer until all the liquid has evaporated.

EXTRAS: Baby marrow slices, marinated sun-dried tomatoes or marinated roasted brinjals; chopped spring onions and parsley mixed with chopped garlic and extra olive oil; and pitted black olives and crumbled feta cheese.

VARIATION 2: Make hotdog rolls (panini, mini Portuguese rolls or ciabatta make a nice change) with braaied boerewors, rocket and a generous spoonful of chilli-tomato jam.

EXTRA: Mash avocado and mix with sour cream and a little lemon juice. Put the braaied boerewors in the bread rolls and serve with a generous spoonful of the avocado mixture and onion sprouts.

Tortilla rolls

Wrap braaied boerewors in a flour tortilla along with plenty of lettuce leaves, cucumber pieces and fresh coriander. Add a dollop of plain yoghurt flavoured with cumin. *[pg 100, bottom]*

Wors nibbles

Braai boerewors, cut into bite-sized pieces and skewer onto cocktails sticks. Serve with instant mustard dressing (prepared mustard mixed with smooth cottage cheese and yoghurt), as well as a selection of pestos mixed with a little mayonnaise and plain yoghurt.

couscous delight

Mix pieces of braaied boerewors with cooked couscous flavoured with a few spoonfuls of chermoula (North African spice). Sauté 2 chopped red peppers and 1 onion sliced into rings in a little oil until soft. Add plenty of fresh coriander and mix with the couscous.

Boerewors and bean salad

Mix pieces of braaied boerewors with 2 cans (410 g each) drained butter beans. Add plenty of chopped fresh parsley and spring onions, pitted black olives, sliced portobello mushrooms, 1 red pepper cut into strips and cherry tomatoes. Moisten with mustard vinaigrette (pg 164). *[pg 100, top]*

'Chicken was not readily prepared on the braai when I was a child, but the smell of pot-roasted chicken brings back fond memories. Times change, and today chicken is frequently on the menu for a braai.'

wholesome

Chicken

When you want a break from red meat, chicken is a great alternative, especially if cooked over the coals until crispy on the outside and juicy and tender inside. You can braai either a whole chicken or chicken pieces over the fire — even a Christmas turkey is delicious cooked over the coals.

GENERAL TIPS

- A whole chicken has an awkward shape, which means it takes quite a while to cook over the coals. The secret is to first brown it over hot coals and then to braai it over lower heat by raising the grid or moving the chicken to the edge of the grid. Alternatively, you can remove some of the hot coals underneath the chicken. It also helps to braai it breast side up for longer so the meat doesn't dry out. To ensure the meat is evenly cooked, it's best to butterfly the chicken and flatten it slightly.
- A whole chicken that's not butterflied is best cooked on a spit. If you have a kettle braai it's even easier. Alternatively, cover the chicken with a double layer of aluminium foil or a dome lid while cooking.
- If using chicken pieces, turn them from time to time and take care not to burn them, especially if the meat has been marinated or you're basting it with a sweetish braai sauce.
- Chicken breasts must be braaied rapidly – if overdone they are dry and tasteless.
- Marinate skinned chicken breasts or baste them while braaiing. Arrange on the grid and braai rapidly over hot coals until just done and not dry. Brush with the marinade from time to time.
- Many cooks swear by parboiling the chicken on the stove until halfway cooked to shorten the braai time. You can roast chicken pieces in the oven at 160 °C for about 30 minutes or slowly bake them in a marinade or chicken stock mixed with a little wine. Braai rapidly over hot coals until brown and crispy on the outside.

QUICK TEST FOR DONENESS

Wiggle the chicken drumsticks in the sockets. If they move easily the chicken is done. Alternatively, prick the thickest part of the meat – usually the thigh – with a meat skewer; if the meat juices run clear the chicken is done. Gently separating the thigh from the body to check the meat is no longer pink inside is also a good way of testing for doneness.

BRAAI GUIDE

Cut	Weight	Cooking time	Internal temperature
Chicken, whole	1.5–1.75 kg	1–1½ hr	82 °C
Chicken, butterflied	1.5–1.75 kg	40–50 min.	82 °C
Chicken breasts, on the bone	225 g	30–35 min.	82 °C
Chicken breasts, deboned	115–150 g	10–12 min.	82 °C
Chicken drumsticks and thighs	115–150 g	35–45 min.	82 °C
Chicken wings	75 g	20–30 min.	82 °C
Poussin	350–450 g	45–60 min.	82 °C
Whole turkey	5–7 kg	2–3 hr	82 °C

CHICKEN PIECES

Curry chicken

MARINADE: Heat the oil in a pan and sauté the onion and garlic until soft. Add the spices and stir-fry for about 2 minutes. Remove from the heat and stir in the chutney, lemon juice and zest. Cool and stir in the yoghurt and mayonnaise.

CHICKEN: Remove any excess skin and fat from the chicken pieces and season with salt and pepper. Put the chicken in a bowl and pour over half the marinade, ensuring the meat is completely covered. Cover and marinate overnight, or for at least 2–3 hours. Braai the chicken over medium coals until done (pg 104), basting from time to time with the remaining marinade used to marinate the chicken. Blend the reserved marinade with the 150 ml yoghurt and stir in the coriander. Spoon the sauce over the braaied chicken or serve separately. Serve with fresh melon slices and basmati rice.

SERVES 6.

TIP: This marinade is also a winner with a whole chicken.

INSTANT TIP – CHICKEN SALAD: Fry deboned chicken breasts and cut into strips. Mix with mayonnaise blended with plain yoghurt. Season with prepared mustard or a pinch of cumin or paprika and serve on a bed of lettuce leaves and sliced banana or diced pineapple, mango, melon or cucumber. Scatter with fresh coriander and chopped cashew nuts before serving.

MARINADE

30 ml olive or cooking oil

1 large onion, chopped

1 clove garlic, crushed

2 ml cayenne pepper

20 ml mild curry powder

5 ml ground coriander

5 ml ground cumin

60 ml chutney

juice and grated zest of 1 lemon

450 ml plain yoghurt

300 ml mayonnaise

CHICKEN

1 kg chicken pieces

salt and freshly ground black
   pepper to taste

150 ml plain yoghurt

30 ml chopped fresh coriander

The chicken is marinated in a mild yet fragrant curry and yoghurt sauce.
The recipe makes a large quantity of sauce but set half aside
and serve with the cooked chicken.

Braaied Greek chicken

1 kg chicken pieces

MARINADE
250 ml plain yoghurt
30 ml lemon or lime juice
3 cloves garlic, crushed
15–30 ml chopped fresh oregano
   or basil
5–10 ml paprika (optional)
salt and freshly ground black
   pepper to taste

Remove any excess skin and fat from the chicken pieces.

MARINADE: Mix all the marinade ingredients and marinate the chicken pieces overnight.

Braai the chicken pieces over medium coals (pg 104) for about 35 minutes, or until done and brown on the outside. Baste with the marinade from time to time. Serve with a salad and freshly baked bread and olive oil. *[pg 107]*

SERVES 4–6.

Lemon juice, garlic and herbs impart a wonderful fresh flavour to this simply cooked roast chicken.

TIP: If you can't find fresh herbs stir a little basil or even sun-dried tomato pesto (available in sachets) into the marinade.

SERVING SUGGESTION – STUFFED PITAS: Use any leftover chicken and shred it. Mix with a little mayonnaise and/or sour cream until well moistened. Also stir in a generous spoonful of sun-dried tomato pesto. Cut open the pitas, stuff with lettuce leaves and spoon the chicken mixture on top.

VARIATIONS – EASY SWEET 'N SOUR BASTING SAUCE: Mix 125 ml honey and 125 ml balsamic vinegar and brush the chicken with the mixture while braaiing. You can also marinate the chicken in the mixture.

EASY SOY SAUCE BASTING SAUCE: Mix 40 ml soy sauce, 1 chopped clove garlic and 20 ml sesame seed oil and brush the chicken with the mixture while braaiing.

Braaied Greek chicken with brown rice salad

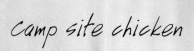

camp site chicken

Mayonnaise chicken

All the mayonnaise chicken recipes published in YOU *over the years have been winners. This one is no exception.*

Remove any excess fat and skin from the chicken pieces, season them with salt and pepper and arrange in a stainless steel dish.

SAUCE: Mix all the sauce ingredients and pour over the chicken. Marinate for at least 30 minutes before braaiing over medium coals for 35–45 minutes or until juicy and done. Serve with pot bread (pg 158) and a salad.

SERVES 4–6.

1 kg chicken pieces
salt and freshly ground black
  pepper to taste

SAUCE
180 ml tomato sauce
10 ml brown sugar
3 ml Tabasco sauce
20 ml ready-made mild mustard
  sauce
20 ml Worcestershire sauce
20 ml brown vinegar
10 ml garlic flakes
100 ml mayonnaise or salad cream

Camp site chicken

Remove any excess fat and skin from the chicken pieces, season them to taste and arrange them in a dish. Mix the mayonnaise and yoghurt and add the cumin. Marinate the chicken in the mixture for about 30 minutes. Braai over medium coals until done (pg 104). *[pg 108]*

chicken pieces, preferably wings
salt and freshly ground black
  pepper to taste
mayonnaise
plain yoghurt
ground cumin to taste

The easiest way to add instant flavour to chicken is to brush it with flavoured mayonnaise. We first tried it at an overnight stop near Nelspruit on the way to the Kruger National Park. Chicken wings work especially well with this recipe.

Mustard chicken

While on an unforgettable trip to the Witsand Nature Reserve in the Kalahari we soon discovered you can cook anything over the coals – even this popular mustard chicken dish was ready in no time. Cook it in a large pan over the fire.

extra sunflower oil

2 onions, cut into chunks

6 chicken thighs, parboiled in
   chicken stock

SAUCE

125 ml sugar

25–50 ml mustard powder

60 ml cake flour

2 ml salt

50 ml sunflower oil

125 ml brown vinegar

250 ml mayonnaise

250 ml boiling water

SAUCE: Blend the sugar, mustard powder, cake flour, salt, oil and vinegar until smooth. Add the mayonnaise and boiling water and mix well.

Pour a little of the extra oil into a large fireproof pan and fry the onions and chicken thighs until brown and done. Pour over the sauce, cover the pan with a lid and heat until the sauce has set slightly. Serve with a salad and bread or baked potatoes.

SERVES 4–6.

Thai chicken

I never go on holiday without packing in a few cans of coconut milk. It gives food a wonderfully exotic flavour. But remember, coconut milk contains saturated fat and is extremely rich so rather opt for the 'lite' variety.

4–6 chicken pieces, preferably
   breasts

coarse salt

MARINADE

2 cloves garlic, crushed

15–30 ml chopped fresh coriander

15 ml chopped fresh mint

10 ml ground cumin

10 ml ground coriander

1 red chilli, seeded and chopped

1 stem lemon grass, chopped, or
   the juice and zest of 1 lemon

10 ml soft brown sugar

250 ml coconut milk

Remove any excess fat and skin from the chicken pieces. Make 3–4 shallow incisions in the meat and arrange the pieces in a dish.

MARINADE: Mix all the marinade ingredients. Pour over the chicken and leave to stand for at least 1 hour.

Braai the chicken over medium coals for about 30 minutes, or until done. Baste with the marinade from time to time. Season with salt. Serve with sticky rice, lemon slices and coleslaw seasoned with Eastern salad dressing (pg 165).

SERVES 4–6.

Tandoori chicken

The word 'tandoori' refers to the clay oven (tandoor) in which this Indian dish is traditionally cooked. You can also make it in a clay or black cast-iron pot buried under hot coals next to the braai fire – similar to how you would make pot bread next to the fire. Alternatively, you can braai the chicken over the coals.

Remove any excess fat and skin from the chicken pieces. Make a few incisions in the thick part of the meat and arrange the pieces in a dish. Sprinkle with lemon juice and coarse salt and leave to stand for 30 minutes.

MARINADE: Mix all the marinade ingredients or blend them to a smooth paste in a food processor. Spoon the mixture over the chicken pieces and mix well. Cover and marinate for at least 1 hour, but preferably overnight.

Braai the chicken pieces over medium coals or bake them in a clay pot until done. Serve with hot naan bread, plain yoghurt mixed with a little finely chopped fresh coriander and lemon wedges. *[pg 111]*

SERVES 4–6.

HOW TO COOK CHICKEN IN A CLAY POT IN THE GROUND:
Soak the clay pot in water for 24 hours before use. Dig a hole in the ground and cover the bottom with hot coals. Stand the pot on bricks over the coals, cover and spoon more coals on top. Bake the chicken for 40–60 minutes, or until done.

8–12 chicken pieces
juice of 1 lemon
coarse salt

MARINADE
250 ml plain yoghurt
1 onion, finely chopped
3 cloves garlic, crushed
2 cm piece fresh ginger, grated
30 ml turmeric
1 green chilli, seeded and chopped
15 ml garam masala

Mexican chicken

WINGS

Finger-licking good – that's the best way to describe chicken wings. They're quick and easy to braai and serve as a snack while waiting for the rest of the meat to cook. Served with a salad and crusty bread they also make a satisfying main course.

Sticky chicken wings

BASTING SAUCE: Mix all the ingredients together.

Arrange the chicken wings on a braai grid and braai for 20–30 minutes, or until done. Baste generously with the sauce from time to time.

SERVES 5–6.

TIP: You can also thread the chicken wings onto kebab skewers (2 wings per skewer) and braai them. If desired, insert a rolled-up bacon rasher between the wings.

16 chicken wings

BASTING SAUCE
125 ml lemon juice
125 ml soy sauce
80 ml smooth apricot jam
80 ml chutney
3 cloves garlic, crushed
1 large onion, finely chopped

Sweet chilli and tomato chicken wings

BASTING SAUCE: Mix all the sauce ingredients.

Arrange the wings on a braai grid and braai for 20–30 minutes, or until done. Baste with the sauce from time to time.

SERVES 4.

6–8 chicken wings

BASTING SAUCE
45 ml olive oil
juice of 1 lemon
45 ml sweet chilli sauce
7 ml paprika
25 ml tomato paste
2 cloves garlic, crushed

Chinese chicken wings

BASTING SAUCE: Blend all the sauce ingredients. Arrange the chicken wings on a braai grid and braai for 20–30 minutes, or until done. Baste with the sauce from time to time. Sprinkle the cooked chicken wings with sesame seeds.

SERVES 4.

TIP: To make a hot sauce, add a little Tabasco to the basting sauce.

TIP: Brush the chicken wings with a sweet 'n sour braai sauce (pg 123) or lemon and honey mixture while braaiing.

6–8 chicken wings
sesame seeds, toasted

BASTING SAUCE
15 ml sesame oil
80–125 ml honey
30 ml wholegrain mustard (optional)
5–7 ml curry powder or Chinese
 five-spice powder
45 ml soy sauce

BREASTS

Braaied chicken breasts are ideal for those on a low-fat diet. But because the breasts contain no fat they can easily become dry while braaiing. Prevent this by braaiing the breasts rapidly – 10–12 minutes (for deboned breasts) is all it takes – and basting them from time to time.

Cajun chicken

The spice mixture is blackened over the fire, giving the chicken a char-grilled appearance.

6 chicken breasts, skinned and
    deboned
cooking oil
Cajun spice mix (pg 13)

Flatten the chicken breasts with the heel of your hand until about 5 mm thick. Brush with oil and lightly roll them in the spice mix. Chill for about 15 minutes to prevent the spice mix from falling off while braaiing. Rapidly braai the chicken breasts over hot coals for 10–12 minutes, or until the spices are blackened and the meat is cooked through. Take care not to overcook the breasts or they will be dry. Serve with sweet 'n sour cucumber salad (pg 169).

SERVES 4–6.

Mexican chicken

Go Mexican and serve braaied chicken breasts with a tomato salsa (below), avocado slices and tortilla chips.

4 chicken breast fillets

BASIC MARINADE
60 ml lemon juice
60 ml olive or cooking oil
3 ml chopped fresh oregano
5 ml finely chopped garlic

MARINADE: Mix all the marinade ingredients. Reserve 45 ml and pour the rest over the chicken. Marinate for 1 hour.

Braai the chicken over hot coals for 10–12 minutes, or until done but not dry. Baste with the marinade from time to time. *[pg 112]*

SERVES 4.

Tomato salsa

45 ml basic marinade (above)
1 tomato, peeled and chopped
60 ml pitted and finely chopped
    black olives
1 small chilli, seeded and finely
    chopped
15 ml chopped fresh coriander
15 ml chopped fresh mint
salt and freshly ground black
    pepper to taste

Mix all the salsa ingredients and serve with the braaied chicken.

SERVES 4.

Chicken breasts with cheese stuffing

Deboned and skinned chicken breasts are ideal for stuffing. Ricotta cheese (a soft low-fat cheese) is perfect for this purpose because it has a neutral taste and adds body to the stuffing, to which you can add any ingredients of your choice. Alternatively, use feta cheese.

Put the chicken breast fillets in a bowl and marinate them in the basic marinade for about 1 hour. Using a sharp knife, cut a pocket crossways in each fillet, but do not cut all the way through. Season with salt and pepper. Insert a piece of spinach leaf in each pocket.

STUFFING: Mix all the stuffing ingredients and divide the mixture among the 4 fillets. Secure the openings with cocktail sticks and braai the stuffed fillets over hot coals for 12–15 minutes, or until just done but not dry. Baste with the marinade from time to time.

SERVES 4.

VARIATION: Blanch about 3 handfuls of young spinach leaves in a saucepan of boiling water until wilted. Squeeze out excess liquid and chop finely. Add 1 wheel of feta cheese (crumbled), 4 chopped piquant peppers and soy sauce to taste. Stuff the chicken breasts with the mixture.

4 chicken breast fillets, skinned
   and deboned
basic marinade (pg 9)
salt and freshly ground black
   pepper to taste
2 young spinach leaves, halved

STUFFING
60 ml ricotta cheese
20 ml sun-dried tomato or basil
   pesto, olive tapenade or a
   mixture of chopped fresh
   herbs such as parsley, oregano
   and chives
1 clove garlic, crushed
juice of 1 lemon (optional)

Spicy chicken

This chicken is fairly hot, so if you prefer your food less fiery omit the chilli powder. You need a large pan to make this dish as the bottom of the pan is deglazed with the liquid ingredients that are then reduced to make a wonderfully fragrant sauce. Look out for pans or woks with feet – they're ideal for setting over coals. A pan on a stand also works well.

Melt the butter in a pan over the coals and fry the chicken breasts, skin side down, along with the garlic until tender and done. Remove from the pan and keep warm. Add the vinegar, wine and chicken stock to the pan and bring to the boil while stirring continuously to deglaze the pan. Add the sun-dried tomato pesto and chilli powder and simmer to reduce to a fragrant, slightly thickened sauce. Add the parsley and spoon over the cooked chicken. Delicious served with crusty bread for mopping up the sauce.

SERVES 3–4.

30 ml butter
4 deboned chicken breasts,
   preferably with skin intact
2 cloves garlic, finely chopped
30 ml balsamic vinegar
60 ml dry white wine
60 ml chicken stock
15 ml sun-dried tomato pesto
1 ml chilli powder
30 ml chopped fresh flat-leaf
   parsley

Eastern chicken

A tasty variation on spicy chicken.

4 deboned chicken breasts,
   preferably with skin intact
salt and freshly ground black
   pepper to taste
2 cloves garlic, finely chopped
30 ml butter
10 ml grated fresh ginger
1 chilli, seeded and chopped
5 ml ground coriander
125 ml chicken stock
juice and zest of 1 lemon
fresh coriander

Season the chicken breasts and fry with the garlic in the butter in a pan set over coals until lightly browned (but not done). Remove from the pan. Stir-fry the ginger, chilli and coriander in the remaining butter for 1 minute, or until fragrant. Return the chicken to the pan and add the stock, lemon juice and zest. Reduce the heat and simmer until done and fragrant. Scatter with fresh coriander and serve with rice.

SERVES 4.

VARIATION: Use chicken wings instead of chicken breasts.

BUTTERFLIED CHICKEN

Braai chicken

The delicious braai sauce is made from basic ingredients.

1 whole chicken, butterflied
salt and freshly ground black
   pepper to taste
2 onions, chopped
cooking oil
30 ml honey
juice of 1 lemon
125 ml tomato sauce
15 ml Worcestershire sauce
125 ml chutney

Season the chicken with salt and pepper. Sauté the onions in a little oil until soft. Add the remaining ingredients and brush the chicken with the mixture. Braai the chicken over medium coals (pg 104) for 50–60 minutes, or until done. Baste with the braai sauce from time to time. *[pg 117]*

SERVES 4.

TIP: Ina Paarman cooks butterflied chicken halfway in the microwave oven before putting it over the coals. Put the chicken, breast side down, in a microwaveproof dish. Do not cover it. Microwave on 65 per cent power for 20–23 minutes and leave to stand for 10 minutes. Cut 3 deep incisions down to the bone in the thighs and breast. Pour over your favourite marinade, cover and marinate in the fridge for at least 6 hours, or overnight. Braai the chicken, breast side up, over medium coals until brown on the outside. Baste with the marinade from time to time.

HOW TO BUTTERFLY A CHICKEN
Using kitchen scissors, cut open the chicken on both sides of the back bone and remove the bone. Put the chicken skin side up on an even surface and flatten the breast with the palm of your hand. Insert two kebab skewers crossways in the butterflied chicken to ensure it retains its shape while cooking.

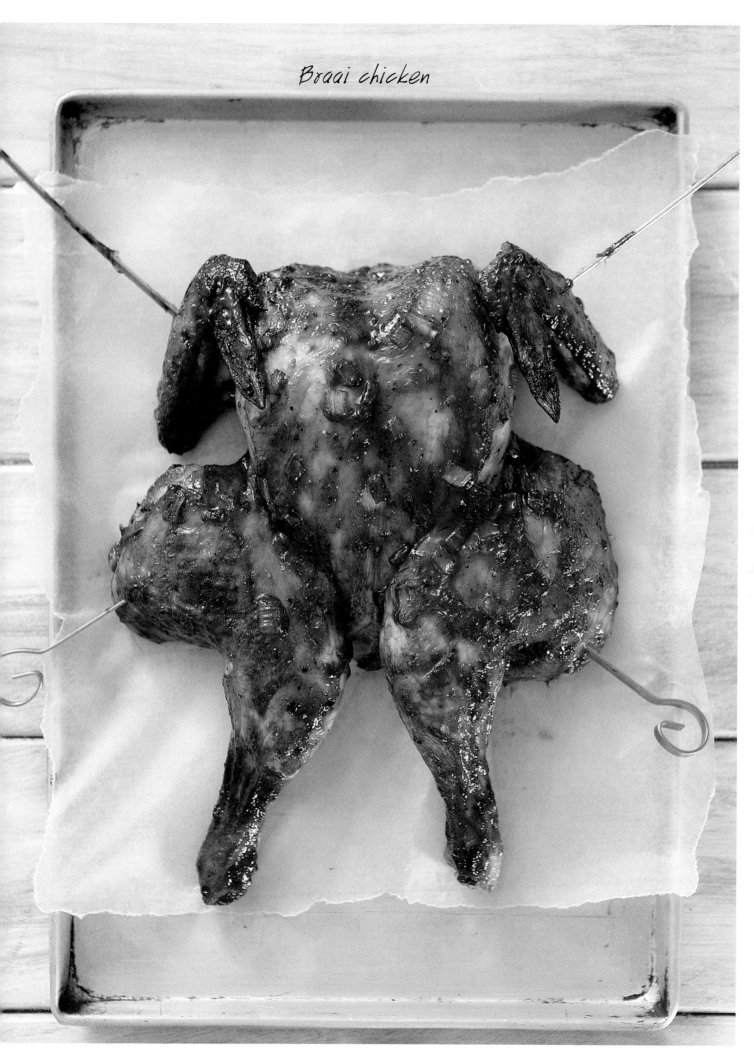

Braai chicken

Butterflied chicken with fragrant butter

2 small chickens, butterflied

FRAGRANT BUTTER
200 g butter (not margarine)
± 3 fresh chillies, seeded and finely
  chopped
20 ml olive or cooking oil
20 ml fresh lemon juice
4 cloves garlic, crushed
10 ml paprika
salt and freshly ground black
  pepper to taste

BUTTER: Mix all the ingredients for the flavoured butter to make a paste. Lift the skin over the breastbone of each chicken and insert a little of the flavoured butter under the skin. Spread the outside of the chickens with the remaining butter and leave to stand for about 2 hours. Braai the chicken over medium coals and serve with peri-peri sauce.

SERVES 6.

Peri-peri sauce

Heat 40 ml butter and stir-fry 4 crushed cloves garlic. Add 2–3 chopped fresh chillies to taste, the juice of 2 lemons and chopped fresh parsley. Serve with chicken.

Africa chicken with chickpea stew

When South African deli queen, Melissa van Hoogstraten of Melissa's in Cape Town, entertains on a large scale she often makes this dish because it goes a long way. Prepare the chicken the day before as it must marinate overnight in chermoula, a fragrant North African paste that's spicy rather than hot. I've provided a recipe for chermoula but you can also buy it ready-made. Alternatively, use smoked paprika – it also imparts a wonderful flavour to the chicken.

2 x 1.5 kg chickens, butterflied
  (or chicken pieces)
salt and freshly ground black
  pepper to taste
30 ml olive oil
250 g chermoula (bought or
  home-made, pg 13)

Season the chickens with salt and pepper. Mix the olive oil with the chermoula and spread over the skin side of the chicken. Put the chicken in a stainless steel dish, cover with clingfilm and marinate overnight. Braai the chicken for 40–50 minutes over medium coals (pg 104), or until the juices run clear. Baste with the marinade mixture from time to time. Serve with chickpea stew (pg 119).

SERVES 10.

TIP: Substitute 10–20 ml smoked paprika mixed with the olive oil for the chermoula.

chickpea stew

Heat the olive oil in a pan and fry the onions and garlic until soft. Add the spices and stir-fry for about 1 minute, or until fragrant. Add the tomatoes, tomato paste, honey and lemon juice and simmer over low heat for about 10 minutes, or until thickened and fragrant. Season with salt and pepper and add the chickpeas. Heat through and spoon onto a large serving platter. Put the braaied chickens on top and garnish with coriander or parsley. *[pg 119]*

SERVES 10.

VARIATION – CHORIZO CHICKPEA STEW: Fry 1 onion and 4 cloves garlic in a little oil until soft. Remove the skins of 200 g chorizo sausages, chop the meat finely and add to the pan. Brown lightly and season with a pinch of cayenne pepper. Add 1 can (400 g) peeled tomatoes and simmer until fragrant. Add 1 can (410 g) chickpeas and season with salt, pepper and a handful of chopped fresh parsley.

olive oil
2 onions, finely chopped
10–15 cloves garlic, crushed
10 ml ground cumin
5 ml ground cinnamon
10 ml turmeric
5 ml paprika
2 cans (410 g each) whole
  tomatoes
20 ml tomato paste
10 ml honey
10 ml lemon juice
salt and freshly ground black
  pepper to taste
2 cans (410 g each) chickpeas,
  drained
fresh coriander or parsley sprigs
  to garnish

WHOLE CHICKEN AND QUAILS

You can also use any of the sauces on pg 123 for added flavour.

TIP: A whole chicken that has not been butterflied cooks most evenly on a spit.

Lemon and herb chicken

This chicken is best cooked in a kettle braai (pg 8), surrounded with potatoes and whole garlic bulbs.

1 whole chicken
salt and freshly ground black
   pepper to taste
1 lemon
2 cloves garlic, crushed
fresh thyme, leaves stripped
10 ml wholegrain mustard
80–100 g butter, softened
1 kg potatoes, scrubbed
extra butter
coarse salt
fresh rosemary sprigs
2 whole garlic bulbs

Make 3 incisions in the thighs and season the chicken inside and out with salt and pepper. Grate the zest of the lemon and mix with the garlic, thyme, mustard and butter. Lift the skin over the breastbone and insert some of the mixture underneath the skin. Put the lemon and a few more fresh thyme sprigs in the cavity of the chicken. Braai over medium coals (pg 104) while brushing the outside of the chicken with the remaining butter mixture from time to time. Meanwhile, rub the potatoes with extra butter and coarse salt and wrap them in aluminium foil along with a few rosemary sprigs. Also rub the garlic with butter and wrap in aluminium foil. Put alongside the chicken over the coals and cook until soft and done. Cut a cross in the top of each potato and press gently to open. Press the cooked garlic purée from the garlic bulbs and spread over the potatoes. Serve with a salad and fresh bread. *[pg 120]*

SERVES 4.

Quails in vine leaves

Laetitia Prinsloo of the Institute of Culinary Arts in Stellenbosch made us these delicious quails over the coals. They're threaded onto bay twigs along with lemon slices and thick slices of French bread and braaied over the coals. Wrapping the quails in the vine leaves is not essential but makes the birds look extra special.

MARINADE: Mix all the marinade ingredients and marinate the quails in the mixture for at least 3 hours.

STUFFING: Mix the stuffing ingredients, if using, and spoon into the cavities of the birds.

Heat the olive oil in a large pan over the coals and brown the quails. Wrap each bird in 2 vine leaves and secure with a piece of string. Thread the quails onto bay twigs or long kebab skewers, alternating with the lemon and bread slices and braai for 30–45 minutes over medium coals until done. Serve with caramelised cherry tomatoes.

SERVES 4–6.

TIP: Instead of threading the quails onto bay twigs or kebab skewers, you can cook them on a spit.

6 whole quails
60 ml olive oil
12 vine leaves, washed
3 lemons, cut into thick slices
1 French loaf, cut into thick slices

MARINADE
50 ml red wine
20 ml chicken stock
20 ml balsamic vinegar
2–3 shallots, sliced
1 bay leaf

STUFFING (OPTIONAL)
4 slices white bread (crusts removed), crumbled
100 g pine nuts, toasted and chopped
200 g fresh grapes, chopped (optional)
6 spinach leaves, blanched and finely chopped
salt and freshly ground black pepper to taste

Orange and ginger quails

Season the quails with salt and pepper. Mix the oranges and ginger preserve and stuff the quails with the mixture. Mix the ginger syrup and orange juice and brush the quails with the mixture. Braai over medium coals for 30–35 minutes, or until done, basting with the remaining sauce from time to time. Serve with rice or a creamy risotto.

SERVES 4.

TIP: Use spring chickens or chicken halves (use the preserve, syrup and juice as a basting instead of a stuffing) instead of the quails.

6 whole quails
salt and freshly ground black pepper to taste
2 oranges, roughly chopped
125 ml ginger preserve, roughly chopped
125 ml ginger syrup (reserved from the ginger preserve)
250 ml orange juice

TURKEY

Fresh, locally bred turkeys are now freely available so you no longer have to worry the meat will be dry and tasteless. The specially bred Bronze turkeys have broad breasts marbled with a little fat, making them less dry than frozen turkeys. And if you don't want to cook a whole bird, try the turkey pieces such as breast steaks, fillets and wings. We discovered how versatile turkey is while visiting Piet du Toit on his turkey farm near Middelburg in Mpumalanga. He also proved turkey is outstanding cooked over the coals.

Whole turkey in a kettle braai

If you want to cook a whole turkey over the coals it's best to do it in a kettle braai. This recipe is straightforward: the bird is not stuffed and is simply glazed with an orange and mustard glaze. Here's a step-by-step guide for cooking perfect turkey.

ORANGE AND MACADAMIA BUTTER (OPTIONAL)

100 ml macadamia nuts or walnuts
100 ml soft butter or margarine
10 ml grated orange zest
10 ml chopped fresh thyme

TURKEY

1 fresh turkey (5–7 kg)
salt and freshly ground black
    pepper to taste
3 oranges, halved
10 pickling onions, peeled and
    halved
± 20 macadamia nuts or walnuts
few sprigs fresh thyme
olive or sunflower oil
1 orange (unpeeled), sliced

ORANGE AND MUSTARD GLAZE

100 ml orange marmalade
20 ml orange juice
20 ml prepared mustard

BUTTER: Chop the nuts finely in a food processor. Add the other ingredients and blend. Chill until needed.

TURKEY: Season the turkey inside and out with salt and pepper. Insert the orange halves, pickling onions, nuts and thyme into the cavity. Secure the drumsticks with string. Spread the outside of the bird with olive or sunflower oil. Tuck the wings underneath the bird.

GLAZE: Mix all the ingredients for the glaze and chill until needed.

TO BRAAI THE BIRD: Put a drip tray on the rack in the middle of the kettle braai. Arrange about 60 burnt-out briquettes either side of the drip tray. Put any remaining oranges, onions and nuts in the drip tray. Put the grid on top and put the turkey on the grid directly above the drip tray. Cover with the lid, ensuring the air vents are fully open. If the turkey initially braais too rapidly, briefly close the air vents three-quarters of the way. Open them completely again to ensure the temperature doesn't drop too much or the turkey won't be cooked through. Braai for 2–3 hours, or until done. An hour after the start of the cooking time, secure orange slices to the turkey carcass using cocktail sticks. Baste with the glaze from time to time. Leave the cooked turkey to rest for 30–60 minutes before carving it. Serve with roast sweet potatoes and butternut.

SERVES 10.

TIP: If desired, fold back the neck skin and insert first your fingers and then your hand between the breast and neck skin, carefully loosening the skin. Insert a little of the macadamia butter between the meat and skin and push the neck skin back into position.

BRAAI SAUCES AND MARINADES

Marmalade braai sauce

Grate the zest of the fruit and squeeze out the juice. Mix the zest and juice with the remaining ingredients and baste a whole or butterflied chicken or chicken pieces with the mixture while braaiing.

1 orange
1 lemon
2 large cloves garlic, crushed
125 ml marmalade
20 ml cumin seeds, crushed
5 ml Worcestershire sauce
salt and freshly ground black
   pepper to taste

Sweet 'n sour braai sauce

Blend all the ingredients and spread over a whole chicken or chicken pieces while braaiing.

TIP: An easy-to-prepare sweet 'n sour basting sauce (pg 106) is equally delicious.

15 ml crushed garlic
15 ml grated fresh ginger
60 ml white wine vinegar
60 ml lemon or orange juice
30 ml tomato sauce
60 ml brown sugar
30 ml soy sauce
10 ml prepared mustard
5 ml paprika

Teriyaki marinade

Teriyaki is a sweet 'n sour soy sauce marinade often used in Japanese cuisine to marinate meat and fish.

Mix all the ingredients and marinate the chicken in the mixture or use as a basting sauce while braaiing.

125 ml soy sauce
15 ml brown sugar
60 ml water
45 ml sherry
1 clove garlic, crushed
5 cm piece fresh ginger, grated

'Fish braais are reminiscent of long summer holidays by the sea, catching big waves and clambering over boulders to inspect rock pools.'

Fish and seafood

At Langebaan on the West Coast the entire holiday revolves around the tides: when to collect

bait on the islands that are only exposed during low tide and spending the day at your

favourite gully waiting for the fish to bite. By sunset you return home tired and sunburnt

(that's if you weren't driven off sooner by the wind), ready to cook your catch of the day,

because there's nothing better than a fresh fish done over the coals.

GENERAL TIPS

CLEANING FISH

Wash and gut the fish. There are no hard and fast rules about whether the scales should be removed: some experts insist that a fish done over the coals tastes better with scales than without. Whatever the case, it's easy to remove the skin, scales and all, after the fish comes off the braai.

If you don't intend braaiing your catch whole, then it must be cut into fillets or portions immediately, wrapped in clingfilm and stored in the fridge.

TIPS

- Fresh fish will keep in the fridge for about three days. Try not to freeze fish as this spoils its flavour and texture.
- Remember to brush both the fish and grid with oil before you start braaiing. Also heat the grid beforehand so the fish is seared as soon as it goes on the fire. A hinged grid works best – it makes turning the fish so much easier.
- Never overcook fish – it's done when the flesh is white and opaque. The general tip that fish is done when it flakes easily with a fork is misleading because it also applies to overcooked fish.

BRAAI GUIDE

Fish and seafood	Size	Cooking time
Fish fillets	1 cm thick	3–5 min.
Fish fillets	2 cm thick	5–10 min.
Fish steaks/portions	2.5 cm thick	10–12 min.
Whole fish and fillets	4 cm thick	10–15 min.
Whole fish and fillets	5–6 cm/450 g	15–20 min.
Whole fish and fillets	7.5 cm/1 kg	20–30 min.
Whole fish	1.5 kg	30–45 min.
Whole crayfish	± 900 g	18–20 min.
Crayfish tails	225–275 g	8–12 min.
Prawns with shells	medium	4–5 min.
Prawns with shells	large	5–6 min.
Prawns with shells	extra-large	6–8 min.
Mussels	medium	4–5 min.

MUSSELS

CLEANING (IF YOU'VE HARVESTED THE MUSSELS FROM THE ROCKS YOURSELF)

Fresh mussels must still be alive when you cook them. Discard mussels with broken or cracked shells or open shells that remain open when you tap the shell with a knife. Scrub the shells and cut off any seaweed. Rinse the mussels under cold running water and leave to soak in cold fresh water for 30 minutes. Replace the water frequently to get rid of any sand that the mussels excrete. Rinse the mussels once more.

Once you've cooked the mussels discard those that remain closed. So before you start cooking or braaiing mussels they must all be closed and once they're done they must all be open.

Garlic mussels in the shell

If you want to braai mussels directly over the coals it's easiest to use mussels on the half-shell. These mussels are served with a creamy sauce.

Arrange the mussel halves in a single layer on the braai grid, hollow sides facing up. Mix the remaining ingredients and spoon over each mussel half. Braai the mussels for about 5 minutes, or until heated through. Serve on slices of toasted Italian bread.

SERVES 3–4.

1 packet (500 g) frozen mussels
   on the half-shell
125 ml mayonnaise
100 ml plain yoghurt
grated zest of 1 lemon
60 ml chopped fresh parsley
1–2 cloves garlic, crushed
coarsely ground black pepper

Mussel pot

A mussel pot is ready in a few minutes. Serve with plenty of crusty bread for mopping up the last bit of juice from the pot.

Heat the olive oil in a potjie over the coals and sauté the garlic, spring onions or onion and fennel, if using, until soft. Add the remaining ingredients, including the mussels, cover and heat for 10–12 minutes or until the fresh mussels open or the frozen mussels are heated through. Serve with crusty bread.

SERVES 3–4.

VARIATION: Cook the mussels in Thai marinade (pg 96).

60 ml olive oil
3 cloves garlic, chopped
3 spring onions or 1 onion,
   finely chopped
1 fennel bulb, sliced (optional)
5–10 ml sugar
2–5 ml paprika
juice of 2 lemons
125 ml white wine
extra 125 ml olive oil
± 30 fresh mussels, scrubbed, or
   frozen mussels on the half-shell

Thai curry mussel pot

Need a change from mussels in a wine and cream sauce?
Then try this recipe – the mussels are cooked in a fragrant curried sauce made with coconut milk.

20 ml cooking oil

10 ml sesame oil

2 cloves garlic, crushed

2 red chillies, seeded and
  finely chopped

15 ml grated fresh ginger

2 spring onions, chopped

2 stems lemon grass, hard outer
  sections removed, chopped
  (optional)

20–30 ml Thai green curry paste

1 can (400 g) coconut milk

15 ml fish sauce

5 ml brown sugar

60 ml chopped fresh coriander

± 30 fresh mussels, cleaned
  (pg 127), or frozen mussels
  on the half-shell

Heat the cooking and sesame oils in a potjie over the coals and stir-fry the garlic, chillies, ginger, spring onions and lemon grass until soft. Add the curry paste and stir-fry for another 2 minutes to develop the flavours. Add the coconut milk, fish sauce and brown sugar and simmer for about 10 minutes, or until fragrant. Add the coriander and mussels, cover and simmer for 10–12 minutes, or until fragrant, heated through and all the mussels have opened. Serve with sticky basmati rice mixed with chopped fresh coriander or coconut milk basmati rice (below). *[pg 129]*

SERVES 3–4.

Mussels in wine and cream sauce

Stir-fry 250 ml finely chopped green pepper and leeks in 25 ml butter until soft.
Add 80 ml white wine and 125 ml fresh cream and bring to the boil.
Simmer to reduce and thicken the sauce slightly. Add the mussels and heat through.

Coconut milk basmati rice

Cook 250 ml rice in 1.25 litres boiling salted water until just beginning to soften.
Drain and rinse, then drain again. Heat 160 ml coconut milk, add it to the rice
and cook until the milk is absorbed. Add chopped red chilli, chopped fresh coriander
and chopped onion to taste.

Thai curry mussel pot

PRAWNS

Grilled garlic prawns

Prawns taste best cooked rapidly over the fire in their shells in butter or oil with loads of garlic. The only other ingredient you need is plenty of lemons to squeeze over the prawns. Serve with crusty bread for mopping up the last traces of garlicky butter.

butter and olive oil for frying

4 large cloves garlic, crushed

2 ml paprika

1 kg extra-large prawns in their
   shells, deveined

juice of 1 lemon

2 handfuls chopped fresh parsley

Heat plenty of butter and olive oil in equal quantities in a large pan over the fire. When the butter mixture begins to foam add the garlic and paprika and stir-fry slightly. Add the prawns and fry rapidly for 5–8 minutes over hot coals until the prawns turn pink. Shake the pan from time to time. Squeeze lemon juice over the prawns and scatter the parsley on top. Serve immediately with lemon slices and crusty bread. *[pg 130]*

SERVES 3–4.

VARIATION – HOT AND SPICY PRAWNS: Add a pinch each chilli powder and turmeric and 3 ml black mustard seeds to the pan and stir-fry with the garlic until the seeds begin to pop. Serve with sweet chilli sauce as a dip.

Peri-peri prawns

These prawns are for those who like it hot.

Arrange the prawns in a dish. Mix the remaining ingredients and marinate the prawns in the mixture for about 30 minutes. Braai the prawns over hot coals for 4–8 minutes, or until done. Serve immediately.

SERVES 4.

16–20 large prawns in their shells
2 ml peri-peri powder
5 ml paprika
2 ml ground coriander
2 cloves garlic, finely chopped
10 ml lemon juice
60 ml olive oil
salt and freshly ground black
    pepper to taste

Prawns in tomato sauce

When prawns are cooked in a sauce I prefer to shell them.
Shelled and cleaned frozen prawns are now available from most supermarkets.

Heat the oil in a large pan over the coals and fry the onion and garlic until soft. Add the tomatoes and simmer until fragrant. Season with paprika and salt and pepper to taste. Crumble half the feta cheese over the tomato mixture, stirring until melted. Add the prawns and simmer for 5–8 minutes, or until done. Crumble the remaining feta cheese on top and serve with crusty bread.

SERVES 4.

30 ml oil
1 small onion, chopped
2 cloves garlic, crushed
600 g Roma or plum tomatoes,
    peeled and chopped
2–5 ml smoked paprika
salt and freshly ground black
    pepper to taste
2–3 rounds feta cheese
1 kg frozen prawns, cleaned

TIP: For this recipe the prawns can be braaied directly over the coals – this gives them a delicious smoky flavour. Use prawns in their shells and arrange them in a double-sided grid or thread them onto skewers in threes. Braai over hot coals for 4–6 minutes, brushing them with oil from time to time. Add to the tomato sauce.

TIP: To defrost frozen prawns rinse them rapidly under cold water before cleaning them.

TIP: Smoked paprika is available from stores such as Woolworths. Unlike ordinary sun-dried paprika, smoked paprika is dried over oak fires, thus the wonderful smoky flavour.

TIP – HOW TO REMOVE THE ALIMENTARY CANAL: Cut open the prawn along the back and carefully lift out the canal with the tip of a knife, taking care not to break it or the flesh will be bitter.

CALAMARI

Char-grilled calamari steaks

I've never been fond of deep-fried calamari rings – to my mind they're often tough. But calamari steaks and tubes are a different story: they're seldom tough and are delicious done on the braai or pan-fried.

3–4 calamari steaks

BASTING SAUCE
juice of 1 lemon
80 ml olive oil
3 cloves garlic, crushed
5 ml Dijon mustard
30 ml chopped fresh parsley
5 ml fresh thyme leaves
freshly ground black pepper
   to taste
rocket leaves to serve

Make shallow incisions crossways on both sides of the calamari steaks. Mix the basting sauce ingredients. Arrange the calamari steaks on the braai grid and braai over hot coals for 3–4 minutes at most, or until white and no longer glassy. Brush constantly with the sauce. Serve on rocket and pour over the remaining sauce. Serve with tartare sauce.

SERVES 3–4.

Tartare sauce

Mix 250 ml mayonnaise, 2 chopped hard-boiled eggs, 10 ml Dijon mustard, 10 ml chopped fresh parsley, 10 ml snipped chives and 10 ml chopped cocktail gherkins or capers, and season with salt and freshly ground black pepper.

Stuffed calamari

Mix feta or ricotta cheese with some capers or a spoonful of basil pesto or olive tapenade. Add a handful of pine kernels or shelled pistachio nuts. Stuff cleaned calamari tubes with the mixture (make sure the plastic-like membrane inside the tubes has been removed) and cut a shallow diamond pattern on the outside of the tubes. Secure the openings of the tubes with cocktail sticks and season with salt and freshly ground black pepper. Grease the stuffed calamari tubes and a hinged braai grid with oil. Arrange the calamari in the grid and braai over medium coals for about 5 minutes a side, or until done and tender. Serve with tartare sauce.

TIP: The secret when making calamari is the temperature: the more rapidly you cook it the more tender it will be.

TIP: Soak the calamari in a little milk before cooking it; this will help to tenderise it.

calamari risotto

I had this deliciously rich risotto at award-winning chef Reuben Riffel's restaurant in Franschhoek.

Heat 40 ml of the oil in a large potjie over the coals and sauté the onion and half the garlic until soft. Add the rice and wine, cover and remove from the fire. Steam for 5 minutes. Return to the fire, add 250 ml of the chicken stock and simmer over low heat. Add the remaining stock a little at a time, waiting for the liquid to be absorbed before adding the next quantity of stock. (*Note:* Always add hot stock and just enough to cover the rice.) Heat the remaining olive oil in a large pan and fry the red onion and the remaining garlic until soft. Add the calamari strips and stir-fry for 2–3 minutes, or until white. Add the tomatoes and spinach and heat through. Once the rice is done, add the calamari mixture, butter and Parmesan cheese, and season to taste with salt and pepper. *[pg 133]*

SERVES 4–6.

50 ml olive oil
125 ml chopped onion
30 ml finely chopped garlic
500 ml Arborio rice
250 ml white wine (sauvignon blanc)
750 ml hot chicken stock
1 small red onion, chopped
250 ml strips calamari steak
125 ml sun-dried tomatoes
   in olive oil
125 ml cherry tomatoes
125 ml blanched spinach,
   roughly chopped
60–100 g butter
125 ml freshly grated Parmesan
   cheese
salt and freshly ground black
   pepper to taste

CRAYFISH

Crayfish should preferably be eaten straight from the sea. Frozen crayfish is just not the same. Fresh crayfish can be kept in the fridge for about two days.

PREPARATION: Lay the crayfish on its stomach with the tail extended on a chopping board. Using a sharp knife, cut open the shell down the centre of the back and across the length of the tail. Remove the entrails and rinse the crayfish well. Season the crayfish with salt and freshly ground black pepper and brush with fragrant lemon butter.

LEMON BUTTER: Mix 125 ml melted butter, 60 ml olive oil, the juice of 2 lemons and 4 crushed cloves garlic. Add a little chopped fresh parsley and coriander if desired.

BRAAI: Put the crayfish on an oiled grid, meaty side facing down, and braai over medium coals to brown the meat slightly. Turn the crayfish so the shell is facing down and braai for another 15 minutes, or until the meat is opaque and easily comes away from the shell. Baste with the lemon butter from time to time. Serve with lemon wedges, a mayonnaise sauce mixed with a little pesto or tomato salsa (pg 114).

TIP: You can also pre-cook the crayfish in boiling salted water until done, and then flash-fry it over the coals.

WHOLE FISH

- The best way to braai fish is whole, with the tail and fins intact, on a braai grid over open coals.

- A large, thick fish is best cooked in a kettle braai, or cover it with a thick layer of aluminium foil while braaiing it over the coals.

FISH THAT ARE SUITABLE FOR BRAAIING: Snoek, elf, Cape salmon (geelbek), dageraad, Cape cod (kabeljou), red steenbras, white stumpnose, roman, panga and silver fish. Smaller types such as hottentot, grunter (knorder) and pilchard can also be put on the braai whole but for a much shorter time than bigger fish.

- Fish between 500 g and 1 kg braai perfectly if you make a few slashes in the sides so the dry heat can penetrate the flesh. Put a few sprigs fresh herbs and lemon slices in the cavity.

Whole fish on the braai

At Muisbosskerm, the popular outdoor seafood eaterie near Lambert's Bay on the West Coast, they know how to do fish on the braai. They believe you mustn't remove the scales of a fish when it's cooked over the coals. You should preferably use a hinged braai grid. Put the whole or butterflied fish or fish steaks on the grid and close it. Braai the fish over slow coals, basting it with lemon butter (pg 134) from time to time. Turn the fish frequently, but leave whole or butterflied fish skin side down for the last 10 minutes of the braai time, or until the fish is done and juicy.

Season the fish with salt and pepper and stuff the cavity with the herbs and lemon slices. Brush the fish and grid with oil. Braai the fish for 15–20 minutes a side over medium to hot coals, brushing with the flavoured butter from time to time. Test for doneness by making a small incision in the thickest part of the fish. Slash the sides of the fish and insert sprigs of parsley and dill to garnish. Serve with lemon wedges.

SERVES 6.

1 whole fish (± 2 kg), cleaned
and gutted
salt and freshly ground black
pepper to taste
1 bunch fresh herbs, such as
parsley and chives
lemon slices
oil for brushing the fish and grid
lemon butter (pg 134) or herb and
spice butter (below)
extra parsley and dill to garnish
lemon wedges to serve

Herb and spice butter

Mix all the ingredients and brush the fish with the mixture while cooking. If you prefer your food spicy use this butter instead of lemon butter.

175 g softened butter
30 ml chopped fresh coriander
3 cloves garlic, crushed
7 ml ground cumin
7 ml paprika
½ red chilli, seeded and finely
chopped
finely grated zest of 1 lemon
salt and freshly ground black
pepper to taste

Langebaan chermoula fish

If we catch fresh fish – usually a stumpnose from the Langebaan lagoon – I like to cook it whole by first frying it in a little oil in a huge pan, and then 'bake' it until done. Gut the fish and remove all the fins (including the back fin), except the tail fin. Remove the scales and make three deep slashes in both sides of the fish. Season well with salt and freshly ground black pepper.

Mix a few spoonfuls of chermoula paste (pg 13) with 375 ml mayonnaise and 125 ml plain yoghurt. Brush the fish inside and out with the mixture and leave to stand for about 1 hour in the fridge.

Add 5 ml cumin to 250 ml cake flour and roll the fish in the mixture. Heat oil in a large shallow pan (you can do this over the coals) and fry the fish on both sides until golden brown. Turn carefully with 2 egg lifters. Cover the fish with a sheet of aluminium foil or cover it with the lid of a kettle (or gas) braai and cook it for about 20 minutes longer over medium coals until done, taking care not to overcook the fish. (Alternatively, you can transfer the fish in the pan to the oven and bake it at 180 °C.) Test for doneness; the flesh must be white throughout and no longer glassy. Transfer the fish to a serving platter and scatter fresh coriander on top. We love a red pepper salsa with this dish or delicious mashed potatoes (pg 185).

Red pepper salsa

Halve and remove the seeds of 3 red peppers and arrange on a baking sheet, cut side facing down. Bake at 200 °C until charred in places and the skin begins to blister. Put the peppers in a plastic bag and leave to cool. Remove the skins and dice the flesh or cut it into strips. Add 30 ml chopped fresh coriander, 10 ml sesame oil, 20 ml sunflower or avocado oil and 30 ml rice wine or balsamic vinegar.

Fish with red curry and coconut milk sauce

This sauce has plenty of bite. Do a whole fish on the braai (pg 135) and pour over the sauce once the fish is done.

SAUCE
5–7 ml red curry paste
1 red chilli, seeded and finely
  chopped (optional)
6 curry leaves (optional)
20 ml oil
250 ml coconut milk
15 ml fish sauce
15 ml sugar

Stir-fry the curry paste, chilli and curry leaves (if using) in heated oil for 2 minutes, or until fragrant. Add the remaining ingredients and simmer for 5 minutes, or until fragrant. Pour over the whole cooked fish.

SERVES 4–6.

TIP: Whole fish, especially those with delicate flesh, can be wrapped in aluminium foil before cooking. Fish that can be prepared this way include: roman, panga, stumpnose, hottentot, dageraad, Cape salmon (geelbek), kob and rainbow salmon. This way you retain all the juices but you don't have the smoky flavour when you cook the fish uncovered over the fire. You can, however, remove the foil when the fish is just done and rapidly sear it on the braai over the open coals. Always use heavy-weight aluminium foil brushed liberally with butter or oil to prevent the fish from sticking. Keep the seasoning simple: a little lemon juice or a few drops soy sauce, salt and freshly ground black pepper and a few knobs of butter are all that's required.

Thai fish

Braai any whole fish (scales removed) as described for whole fish on the braai (pg 135), while brushing with lemon butter from time to time. Pour over this deliciously fragrant Thai sauce. Well-known food writer Justine Drake gave us this recipe.

SAUCE

30 ml soy sauce

45 ml lime or lemon juice

15–25 ml brown sugar or
    sweet soy sauce (ketjap manis)

few drops fish sauce

5 ml sesame oil (optional)

1 clove garlic, crushed

5 cm piece fresh ginger, peeled
    and cut into long thin strips

1 bunch fresh coriander, chopped

2 red chillies, seeded and chopped

½ English cucumber, halved,
    seeded and cut into thin strips

2 carrots, scraped and cut into
    thin strips

1 red or yellow pepper, seeded
    and cut into thin strips

salt and freshly ground black
    pepper to taste

Bring all the sauce ingredients to the boil in a saucepan and remove from the heat immediately. Transfer the cooked whole fish to a serving platter and immediately pour over the hot sauce. Serve with basmati rice.

SERVES 4–6.

Fish is everyday food on the West Coast. Snoek is a particular favourite and nothing goes to waste. Snoek roe is pan-fried, while the heads are used to make curry and soup. Rollmops, bokkoms (dried mullet) and dried snoek also appear regularly on the table.

West Coast snoek

I was inducted into the art of how to do a real West Coast snoek braai by three West Coast residents from Saldanha, Myra Stoffberg, Patricia van Schalkwyk and Sharon February. Typical of this region, they like their snoek with something sweet – even the basting sauce is fairly sweet.

1 snoek, butterflied if desired

SAUCE

100 ml sunflower oil

50 ml vinegar or lemon juice

10 ml fish spice mix

30 ml finely chopped garlic

30 ml smooth apricot jam

30 ml chutney

30 ml mayonnaise

2 ml freshly ground black pepper

Wash the snoek, pat it dry and place it on a braai grid.

SAUCE: Mix all the sauce ingredients and microwave the mixture for 2 minutes, or until melted. Braai the snoek for 10–15 minutes a side until just done. Brush with the sauce from time to time while on the braai. Serve with sweet potatoes baked on the fire and toasted sandwiches or freshly baked bread. *[pg 139]*

SERVES 6–10.

TIP: The fish can also be brushed with a mayonnaise or apricot jam sauce. To make the mayonnaise sauce mix 250 ml mayonnaise with 90 ml melted butter and for the apricot sauce blend 60 ml mayonnaise, 60 ml melted garlic butter and 60 ml apricot jam.

Ginger and honey sauce

This sauce for snoek has an exotic Eastern flavour.

50 ml butter

juice and zest of 2 limes

2 cloves garlic, crushed

7 ml grated fresh ginger

30 ml honey

45–60 ml soy sauce

5 ml fish sauce or oyster sauce
   (optional)

handful fresh coriander, chopped

Heat the sauce ingredients in a small saucepan until the butter has melted. Brush the snoek with the sauce while braaiing.

It's easiest to thread small fish onto a skewer. Keep them whole but gut them and insert skewers through the head and tail. They can also be butterflied, rolled and threaded onto skewers in threes.

Mullet (harders) or pilchards on the braai

4–6 whole mullet or pilchards,
   cleaned and gutted (they can also
   be butterflied)

salt and freshly ground black
   pepper to taste

90 ml cooking oil

45 ml lemon juice

coriander and chilli sauce (below)
   (optional)

Make 3 deep incisions in both sides of the fish and season them with salt and pepper. Blend the oil and lemon juice. Thread each fish onto a skewer and braai them over medium coals for 8–10 minutes, turning halfway through the braai time. Brush with the oil and lemon mixture from time to time. Transfer the cooked fish to a serving platter and pour over the coriander and chilli sauce if desired. Leave to stand for 5 minutes so the flavours can be absorbed. Serve with couscous or basmati rice.

SERVES 4–6.

Coriander and chilli sauce

2 shallots, finely sliced

2 cloves garlic, crushed

1 red chilli, seeded and chopped

80 ml olive oil

10 ml sesame oil (optional)

juice and grated zest of 1 lemon

60 ml chopped fresh coriander

30 ml chopped fresh parsley

salt and freshly ground black
   pepper to taste

Mix all the ingredients and pour over the mullet or pilchards.

VARIATION: Blend a little chermoula paste with oil and brush small fish or fish pieces with the mixture while on the braai. Serve with delicious mashed potatoes (pg 185).

TIP: To butterfly pilchards remove the heads, cut the fish open from top to tail and gut them. Rinse the fish under cold water and lay them flat on a work surface, cut side facing down. Press along the backbone to flatten the fish completely. Turn the fish, pull the backbone away from the flesh and snip off at the tail with scissors. Remove any bones that may have been left behind. Braai the fish for 3–6 minutes per side, or until done.

FISH FILLETS

According to author Pieter Pieterse, who spent a long time living in his caravan, Die Spookhuis, next to the West Coast's fishing waters, oily fish such as snoek and hottentot are best for doing over the coals. Drier kinds of fish, such as Cape cod (kabeljou), Cape salmon (geelbek), steenbras, yellowtail and the different kinds of red fish, are best fried in a pan.

Cajun fish

Mix the Cajun spice mix with the cake flour. Roll the fish pieces in the melted butter and then in the spice mix. Arrange the fish on an oiled grid and braai over medium coals for 2–4 minutes per side, or until just done. Serve with skewered potato wedges (pg 182) and guacamole (avocado salsa) (pg 97).

Cajun spice mix (pg 13)
180 ml cake flour
8 white fish pieces, fillets or steaks
125 g butter, melted

SERVES 8.

TIP: Fish fillets must be frequently brushed with melted butter, oil and lemon juice or any other marinade while on the braai. First brown the meaty side of the fish over hot coals then turn so the skin side is facing down and braai over cooler coals until done.

Skottelbraai fish

This is basically a variation of baked fish. I think fish portions or fillets (preferably with skin off) are best cooked in a skottelbraai. You can also do them in a large pan on the fire.

Remember to put a little butter and oil in the pan or the fish will stick to the bottom. I like to add a little fresh garlic and sprinkling of lemon juice to the pan while the fish is frying.

My favourite is fried fish fillets that have been rolled in a little cake flour to make them deliciously crisp on the outside.

Pan-fried fish

Fry fish pieces in a large pan over the coals. Serve with rocket pesto (below) on delicious mashed potatoes (pg 185) if desired. Alternatively, plain chips and plenty of lemon slices are all you need.

4 white fish fillets
salt and freshly ground black
   pepper to taste
cake flour
30 ml butter
30 ml olive oil
fresh lemon juice
chopped fresh parsley

Season the fish with salt and pepper and roll each fillet in the cake flour. Heat the butter and oil in a large pan or skottelbraai until foaming and fry for 2 minutes a side, or until done and golden brown on the outside. Drizzle with a little lemon juice and scatter parsley on top. Serve as suggested above or with spicy tomato sauce or caramelised tomatoes. *[pg 143]*

SERVES 4.

Rocket pesto

1 small clove garlic, crushed
1 small onion, chopped
handful fresh flat-leaf parsley
1 packet (50 g) rocket
juice of 1 lemon
salt and freshly ground black
   pepper to taste
150 ml olive oil

Purée all the pesto ingredients, except the olive oil, in a food processor. Slowly pour the oil through the spout while the machine is running. Blend again and serve with baked fish fillets.

SERVES 4.

Spicy tomato sauce

This spicy tomato sauce is delicious with pan-fried fish.

20 ml oil
1 large onion, sliced
2 cloves garlic, crushed
30 ml garam masala
3 ml turmeric
4 whole cloves
15 ml ground cumin
5 cardamom pods, bruised
2 whole cinnamon sticks
3 large Roma or plum tomatoes,
   peeled and chopped
salt and freshly ground black
   pepper to taste
pinch of sugar

Heat the oil in a pan and stir-fry the onion and garlic until soft. Add all the spices and stir-fry for about 2 minutes, or until fragrant. Add the tomatoes, reduce the heat and simmer for about 10 minutes, or until fragrant. Remove the whole spices and season with salt, pepper and a pinch of sugar.

SERVES 4.

Pan-fried fish

Fish with dukkah crust

Ensure you always have a container of dukkah in the cupboard because it can be used in all kinds of ways.

6 fish fillets, skin removed

fresh lemon juice

salt and freshly ground black
  pepper to taste

olive oil and butter

dukkah

Sprinkle the fish with lemon juice and season with salt and pepper. Heat a little olive oil and butter in a pan or skottelbraai. Braai the fish fillets for about 2 minutes, turn them and sprinkle liberally with dukkah. Braai the fish for another 3–5 minutes, or until just done. Serve with couscous and grilled lemon halves (below). *[pg 144]*

SERVES 6.

TIP – GRILLED LEMON HALVES: Put lemon halves cut side down on the grid and sear.

Marinated fish

Try to marinate fish for a while before putting it on the braai. This marinade is flavoured with smoked paprika, which imparts a special flavour to fish such as tuna, snoek and any white fish. If unobtainable, use about 10 ml ordinary paprika.

Pound the garlic and salt in a mortar and pestle until smooth. Add the lemon juice, onion and spices. Spread both sides of the fish steaks with the mixture and drizzle with a little oil. Braai 2–3 minutes a side, or until just done. Serve with couscous and coarse tomato salsa made with cherry tomatoes, garlic, onion, red pepper, olive oil, chopped fresh coriander, brown sugar and balsamic vinegar, or serve with tzatziki.

SERVES 4.

4 fish steaks
cooking oil

MARINADE
2 cloves garlic, crushed
pinch salt
juice of 1 lemon
1 small onion, grated
3 ml smoked paprika
3 ml ground cumin

FISH PIECES IN ALUMINIUM FOIL

Mediterranean fish in foil

Put each fish fillet on a large sheet of heavy-duty aluminium foil. Season with salt and pepper. Arrange strips of anchovies crossways on top of each fillet, scatter the olives, capers and parsley on top and drizzle with the olive oil. Wrap in the aluminium foil and bake over medium coals for 10–12 minutes, or until just done. Serve with crusty bread, such as ciabatta, and extra olive oil.

SERVES 4.

VARIATION: Sprinkle a layer of thinly sliced leeks on the sheet of aluminium foil and arrange the fish fillets on top. Season with salt and pepper and drizzle with a little olive oil. Top with a slice of lemon, wrap in the aluminium foil and bake until done.

TIP: If you want to brown a dish from the top, cover it with a sheet of heavy-duty aluminium foil and place a layer of coals on top. Check occasionally to see if the dish is turning brown and remove the sheet of aluminium foil with the coals as soon as the dish is ready.

4 thick white fish portions
salt and freshly ground black
    pepper to taste
4 anchovies, halved lengthways
8–10 green olives, pitted and
    chopped
15 ml capers, chopped
60 ml chopped fresh flat-leaf
    parsley
45 ml olive oil

STEWS AND PAELLA

Moroccan fish stew

Mussels and white fish are gently simmered in a fragrant tomato sauce liberally flavoured with paprika and cumin.

15 ml olive oil

1 onion, finely chopped

1 clove garlic, crushed

15 ml paprika

5 ml ground cumin

pinch sugar

1 can (400 g) whole peeled
  tomatoes in their juice, chopped

250 ml vegetable stock

600 g white fish, cubed

1 can (410 g) butter beans, drained

400 g frozen mussels on the
  half-shell

salt and freshly ground black
  pepper to taste

chopped fresh parsley

Heat the oil in a potjie over the coals and stir-fry the onion and garlic until soft. Add the seasonings and stir-fry for 2 minutes. Add the tomatoes and vegetable stock, reduce the heat and simmer for about 10 minutes, or until fragrant. Add the fish and simmer until just done. Add the butter beans and mussels and warm through. Season to taste with salt and pepper and scatter the parsley on top. Serve with white rice.

SERVES 4.

Curried fish potjie

100 m cooking oil

3 onions, chopped

3 cloves garlic, chopped

1 red pepper, seeded and chopped

1 stalk celery, chopped

30–60 ml curry powder

5 ml vinegar

1 kg potatoes, peeled and cubed

salt

water

1 kg white fish (such as hake),
  cubed

1 kg mussels on the half-shell

1 kg calamari tubes or steaks,
  cut into strips

salt and freshly ground black
  pepper to taste

lemon juice

chopped fresh parsley

Heat the oil in a potjie and sauté all the vegetables, except the potatoes, until soft. Sprinkle the curry powder on top and stir-fry lightly. Add the vinegar and potatoes and season with salt. Add just enough water to cook the potatoes until nearly soft. Add the fish and seafood and simmer until just done – not longer than 7–10 minutes. Season with salt and pepper and sprinkle with lemon juice. Scatter parsley on top and serve with rice.

SERVES 10.

Paella

Heat a little oil in a large pan and put it on a stand over the fire. Rapidly fry the prawns until they just turn pink and remove from the pan. Rapidly fry the calamari strips until white, season with salt and pepper and lemon juice while on the braai, and then remove from the pan. Add more oil to the pan and fry the onion, garlic, green pepper, paprika and turmeric until the onion and garlic are soft. Add the sausage and chicken and fry until just done. Season with salt and pepper. Add the rice and mix. Add the tomatoes and vegetable stock, cover and simmer until the rice is soft and most of the liquid has evaporated. Add the peas and mussels and heat through. Return the prawns and calamari to the pan and heat through. Scatter the herbs on top. *[pg 147]*

SERVES 6–8.

TIP: Use a packet of marinara seafood mix instead of the prawns and calamari.

cooking oil

1 packet (200 g) cleaned, frozen prawns

125 g calamari steaks, sliced into strips (optional)

salt and freshly ground black pepper to taste

juice of 1 lemon

1 onion, sliced into rings

2–3 cloves garlic, crushed

1 green pepper, seeded and chopped

5–10 ml paprika

2–5 ml turmeric

1 chorizo sausage, chopped

2 chicken breast fillets, cubed

500 ml uncooked rice

1 can (410 g) chopped tomatoes

1 litre vegetable stock

250 ml frozen peas

250 g frozen mussels on the half-shell

chopped fresh parsley and coriander

'I've never found kneading and baking bread a chore. As children, barely tall enough to peek over the kitchen table, we each got a chance to try our hand at kneading the dough. And because of those memories, I also can't imagine a braai without bread in some form or other. For me, freshly baked slices with real butter and green fig preserve are still the best, but share-bread with olive oil is just as good. Everyone just loves freshly baked bread hot out of the oven or from the fire.'

heavenly Breads and other bakes

Serve it sliced as a starter with spreads or as part of the main meal. If you're not confident enough to bake your own bread try the recipes for picnic loaves with delicious stuffings or the quick-mix loaves that require no kneading. There are also recipes for pot, flat and ash bread so you can experiment with the dough. My mother-in-law, Suzie, taught me to prepare pot bread — and even how to bake it in a hole in the ground. If kneading sounds like too much effort buy ready-made bread dough — your guests will still think you're a master baker!

BREAD SNACKS

Buttermilk griddlecakes

4 x 250 ml cake flour
5 ml bicarbonate of soda
5 ml cream of tartar
5 ml salt
50 ml butter
375 ml buttermilk

Sift together the dry ingredients and rub in the butter. Add the buttermilk and mix to make a stiff dough. Put the dough on a floured surface, break into uniform pieces and shape into rolls. Cut the rolls into 4 cm thick slices, flatten them slightly and leave to rise until double in volume. Toast over the coals or in a hot griddle pan until brown on the outside and cooked inside.

MAKES 8 GRIDDLECAKES.

TIP: If preferred, substitute the bicarbonate of soda and cream of tartar with 20 ml baking powder.

Stuffed bread snacks

Prepare the buttermilk griddlecake dough. Stack a little feta cheese, basil or sun-dried tomato pesto, chopped olives and/or chopped marinated tomatoes on each slice of dough and fold the dough over the filling, pressing it down. Proceed as described. *[pg 150]*

Share-bread

Prepare the buttermilk griddlecake dough. Stack a little feta cheese, basil or sun-dried tomato pesto, chopped olives and/or chopped marinated tomatoes on each slice of dough and fold the dough over the filling, pressing it down. Pack the balls tightly in a greased ring cake tin, leave to rise and bake at 190 °C for 20–30 minutes, or until done. Serve with olive oil blended with balsamic vinegar.

SERVING SUGGESTION: Place crusty loaves with bowls of olive oil and dukkah on the table. Guests can then help themselves to pieces of bread to dip in the oil and then the dukkah.

Quick beer loaf or griddlecakes

Mix 1 packet (500 g) self-raising flour and a pinch salt with just enough water
or beer to make a stiff dough. Divide the dough evenly among 3–4 greased cans
(use any opened 400 g cans), or use a medium loaf tin, and bake in a preheated
oven at 180 °C or until done.

VARIATION: Shape the dough into small balls and flatten them to a thickness of
3 cm. Cut out griddlecakes with a glass and toast over hot coals until done.

Toasted tortillas

Put 4 tortillas on a work surface. Mix the remaining ingredients and divide
among the tortillas. Cover with the remaining tortillas. Put them in a hinged
braai grid and toast over medium coals until the cheese has melted and the
tortillas are lightly browned on the outside.

SERVES 4.

8 tortillas
600 g feta cheese
10 sun-dried tomatoes, chopped
15 ml pitted and chopped black
  olives

SPREADS

Cottage cheese spread

Use about 125 g full-cream cottage cheese as the main ingredient and add one of the following:

- sun-dried tomato, basil or coriander pesto
- olive tapenade
- 10 chopped piquant peppers

Chickpea spread

In a food processor blend 1 can (400 g) drained chickpeas with 15 ml tahini (sesame seed
paste), the juice of 1 lemon, 2 crushed cloves garlic, 45 ml chopped flat-leaf parsley and
10 ml chopped fresh mint. Slowly add 125 ml oil and stir in 250 ml cream cheese.

Brinjal spread

Cut 2 brinjals in half, put them on a greased baking sheet, cut side down, and bake at 190 °C
for 30–40 minutes, or until done. Put the unpeeled brinjals in a food processor, add the
same ingredients as for the chickpea spread (above), excluding the chickpeas, and blend until
smooth. Add 250 ml cream cheese.

Mussel pâté

To make this West Coast speciality, blend 500 g cooked mussels, 1 small chopped onion and
200 ml fresh cream in a food processor. Season with lemon pepper and fish spice to taste.

Picnic loaf

A hollowed-out Italian or sourdough loaf stuffed with roasted or char-grilled vegetables is delicious with a braai. Let guests help themselves to a slice of the veggie-stuffed loaf. Make it the day before so it's firm when sliced.

1 sourdough or Italian loaf, such as ciabatta
olive oil or sun-dried tomato or basil pesto
roasted or char-grilled vegetables, such as brinjal, peppers and baby marrows,
    marinated in herb vinaigrette (pg 164)
12 small or 3 large Roma tomatoes, sliced
300 g mozzarella or feta cheese, sliced

Slice off the top crust of the loaf to make a 'lid' and set aside. Hollow out the inside of the loaf, leaving a ± 1.5-cm-thick rim. Brush the inside of the loaf with olive oil or spread with pesto. Layer the vegetables, tomatoes and cheese inside, cover with the 'lid' and wrap the loaf tightly in aluminium foil. Serve as is with braaivleis or heat over the coals until the cheese has just melted. *[pg 152]*

SERVES 6.

Anchovy and cheese loaf

Marcia Margolius, décor guru, likes to serve this loaf with steak.

250 g Cheddar cheese, grated
15 ml mayonnaise
1 can (410 g) asparagus salad cuts, drained
10 ml Dijon mustard
fresh basil, thyme and dill to taste
1 large French loaf
6 anchovies
extra basil to garnish

Preheat the oven to 180 °C.

Blend the cheese, mayonnaise, asparagus, mustard and herbs in a food processor until smooth. Slice off the top crust of the loaf to make a 'lid' and hollow out the inside of the loaf. Spoon the cheese mixture into the hollowed-out bread and top with the anchovies. Return the 'lid' and wrap the loaf in aluminium foil. Bake in the preheated oven for 25 minutes or until the cheese has melted and the loaf is crusty. Remove the aluminium foil and top crust before serving the loaf. Garnish with basil.

SERVES 4.

Lavache

These crisp, thin sheets are similar to Indian poppadums and are delicious served with a selection of spreads.

Preheat the oven to 180 °C. Line 2 baking sheets with baking paper and spray with non-stick spray. Mix the flour and salt and mix with just enough lukewarm water to make a thick paste. Spread thinly and evenly over the baking paper and sprinkle the spices and garlic on top. Bake in the preheated oven for about 15 minutes, or until golden brown. Cool slightly on the baking sheet before carefully removing from the baking paper. Break into large pieces and serve with a selection of spreads (pg 151).

MAKES 2 SHEETS.

350 ml white bread flour
pinch salt
lukewarm water
biltong spice, paprika, chilli
   and garlic

QUICK-MIX LOAVES

Sweet coconut loaf

Preheat the oven to 180 °C. Line a medium loaf tin with baking paper.

Whisk the eggs, milk and vanilla essence. Sift together the flour, salt, baking powder and cinnamon and add the sugar and coconut. Add the egg mixture and melted butter to the flour mixture and mix well. Turn the dough into the pan and bake in the preheated oven for 45–60 minutes, or until done. Leave the loaf to cool in the tin before carefully turning out.

MAKES 1 MEDIUM LOAF.

2 eggs
400 ml milk
5 ml vanilla essence
625 ml cake flour
pinch salt
10 ml baking powder
10 ml ground cinnamon
250 ml sugar
400 ml desiccated coconut
75 g butter, melted

Steamed mealie meal loaf

A copy of the gorgeous coffee-table book African Salad, *with stories, pictures and recipes from every corner of the country, arrived at the* YOU *test kitchen and we simply had to publish recipes from the book in the magazine. This recipe for a mealie meal loaf steamed in a potjie over the fire comes from the KwaZulu-Natal heartland. The dough is spooned into a colander that is then placed in the pot to ensure the loaf is above the water level.*

Mix the instant yeast and water, add the flour, salt and sugar and mix well. Gradually knead in the mealie meal. Put the dough into a greased colander that fits into a large potjie or saucepan. Leave until well risen. Bring 500 ml water to the boil in the pot and put the colander with the dough inside. Cover, reduce the heat and steam for 1 hour, or until done. *[pg 155]*

SERVES 6.

1 sachet (10 g) instant yeast
250 ml hot water
500 ml white bread flour
2 ml salt
125 ml sugar
350 ml mealie meal

Quick mealie meal loaf

250 ml cake flour
250 ml mealie meal
50 ml sugar
15 ml baking powder
2 ml salt
1 ml chilli powder (optional)
250 ml buttermilk
50 ml oil
50 ml honey
2 eggs, lightly whisked
250 ml whole kernel sweet corn
   (optional)
30 ml finely chopped green pepper
   (optional)

Preheat the oven to 190 °C. Grease a 22 x 10 cm loaf tin, line the base with baking paper and grease with non-stick food spray. Combine the dry ingredients. Mix the buttermilk, oil, honey and eggs and add to the dry ingredients along with the sweet corn and green pepper if using. Turn the dough into the prepared tin and bake in the preheated oven for 20–40 minutes, or until a testing skewer comes out clean. Leave the loaf to cool slightly in the tin before turning out onto a wire rack.

MAKES 1 LOAF.

Raisin loaf

I discovered this recipe on the West Coast. Butter slices of the bread generously and serve with braaied fish.

1 packet (500 g) self-raising flour
125–250 ml sugar
125 ml raisins
pinch salt
1 ml aniseed
1 egg
500 ml milk

Preheat the oven to 180 °C. Grease a medium loaf tin. Combine all the dry ingredients in a mixing bowl. Whisk together the egg and milk and add to the flour mixture. Turn the dough into the tin and bake in the preheated oven for 50–60 minutes, or until a testing skewer comes out clean. Leave the loaf to cool slightly in the tin before carefully turning out onto a wire rack.

MAKES 1 LOAF.

Steamed mealie meal loaf

Seed loaf

Naomi Friis of Philippolis in the Free State treated us to the most delicious home cooking. She experimented with this recipe, tweaking it until perfected.

Preheat the oven to 190 °C. Grease a flat-bottomed potjie or deep 22 cm cake tin. Combine all the dry ingredients. Add the milk, oil and just enough lukewarm water to make a stiff dough and mix with a wooden spoon. Turn the dough into the prepared pot, cover with clingfilm and leave to rise until double in volume. Remove the clingfilm and bake in the preheated oven for about 40 minutes, or until done.

MAKES 1 LARGE LOAF.

625 ml white bread flour
250 ml oats
250 ml wholewheat flour
250 ml bran
80 ml sunflower seeds
80 ml poppy seeds
5 ml salt
25 ml yellow sugar
1 sachet (10 g) instant yeast
250 ml lukewarm milk
25 ml sunflower oil
lukewarm water

Pumpkin seed loaf

Preheat the oven to 190 °C. Combine the cake flour, salt, baking powder, bicarbonate of soda, wholewheat flour, bran and pumpkin seeds. Mix the plain yoghurt or buttermilk and the warm water and stir into the dry ingredients. Divide the dough between 2 greased 1-litre loaf tins and bake in the preheated oven for 45–50 minutes, or until done. Leave the loaves to cool in the oven for 10 minutes before turning out onto a wire rack. The loaves freeze well.

MAKES 2 LOAVES.

500 ml cake flour
5 ml salt
10 ml baking powder
7 ml bicarbonate of soda
750 ml wholewheat flour
500 ml bran
500 ml toasted pumpkin seeds
500 ml plain yoghurt or buttermilk
250 ml warm water

Quick pan pizza

Roll out 500 g ready-made bread dough until thin and press onto a greased baking sheet. Peel and chop 4 plum tomatoes and mix with 45 ml basil or sun-dried tomato pesto. Spread the dough with the tomato mixture and arrange a few rashers of back bacon and vegetables such as baby marrows, cooked butternut, onion slices and mushrooms on top. Grate plenty of mozzarella cheese on top. Bake at 220 °C for 10–12 minutes or until the base is done. Drizzle with olive oil and sprinkle Parmesan cheese on top (or break fresh mozzarella (bocconcini) into pieces and layer on top). Serve immediately. *[pg 156]*

SERVES 4.

KNEADED LOAVES

Pot bread

This basic bread dough is used to bake all kinds of bread. If you like it simple serve the loaf with butter, cheese and jam. If you're feeling more adventurous try it with olive oil and sea salt flakes or dukkah. Alternatively, pour a creamy sauce over the uncooked loaf or knead grapes, olives, cheese or onion into the dough and make a pot or flat bread.

Basic bread dough

700 g (5 x 250 ml) white bread flour
1 sachet (10 g) instant yeast
5 ml salt
60 ml cooking or olive oil
500 ml lukewarm water

Preheat the oven to 190 °C. Grease a 25 cm flat-bottomed potjie and lid with margarine.

Sift together the dry ingredients. Add the oil and just enough lukewarm water to make a stiff dough. Knead for about 10 minutes, or until smooth and elastic. Brush the surface of the dough with oil, cover with clingfilm and leave in a warm place to rise until double in volume.

Knock down the dough. Pinch off small balls of the dough and arrange in the prepared pot. Cover with the lid and leave in a warm place to rise again until double in volume. Bake in the preheated oven for about 1 hour, or until brown and done and the loaf sounds hollow when tapped.

MAKES 1 LARGE LOAF.

HOW TO BAKE BREAD IN THE GROUND
Make a hollow in the ground, fill with a few hot coals, arrange bricks on either side of the coals and put the pot on top. Put a few coals on top of the lid.

TIP: If you don't feel like kneading the dough, buy ready-made bread dough and bake any of the delicious loaves described here.

Pot bread with tomato and cheese-cream sauce

Prepare the basic bread dough, leave to rise, and then knock it down. Break the dough into balls and arrange them in the prepared potjie (pg 158). Leave to rise again until double in volume. Preheat the oven to 190 °C.

SAUCE: Fry the bacon in a pan until done. Add the tomato and onion mix and reduce slightly. Add the cream, season with salt and pepper and simmer until slightly reduced and fragrant. Pour the sauce over the risen dough, sprinkle with the cheese and bake in the preheated oven for about 1 hour or until the bread is done. Remove the lid for the last 15 minutes. Serve lukewarm.

SERVES 6–8.

1 x basic bread dough (pg 158)

SAUCE
½ packet (125 g) shoulder bacon, chopped
1 can (400 g) tomato and onion mix
250 ml fresh cream
salt and freshly ground black pepper to taste
250 ml grated Cheddar cheese

Grape loaf

Prepare the bread dough as described and leave to rise. Add rosemary, grapes and nuts to the dough when you knock it back. Place the dough in a greased loose-bottomed tin. Leave to rise until double in size.

Preheat the oven to 190 °C. Sprinkle the dough with a little salt and castor sugar and bake for about 1 hour in the preheated oven, or until done. Serve with Brie cheese or lemon butter (see tip below) and fish as desribed below.

SERVES 6–8.

VARIATION: Simmer 200 g seedless raisins in 250 ml muscadel until syrupy. Halve the dough and roll out each half. Place one half on a baking sheet, spoon the filling on top and cover with the other half. Pinch the edges together and press the grapes (and nuts, if using) into the surface of the dough. Leave the dough to rise and bake until done.

TIP – LEMON BUTTER: Mix 125 g softened butter with 5 ml grated lemon zest, 15–30 ml lemon juice and a pinch chilli flakes.

1 x basic bread dough (pg 158, use olive oil)
15 ml chopped fresh rosemary
500 g seedless black grapes
50 g halved pecan nuts (optional)
sea salt flakes and castor sugar for sprinkling on top

Serve this grape loaf with braaied fish or as a starter with dried bokkoms.

Cheese and onion flat bread

Deliciously tempting! Sweet 'n sour onions and cheese mixed into the bread dough – you can't get enough of this bread. Let guests break off pieces of the bread and dip them in olive oil.

1 x basic bread dough (pg 158)
125–200 ml crumbled feta or
    blue cheese

CARAMELISED ONIONS
2 onions (preferably red), sliced
30 ml olive oil
30 ml brown sugar
45 ml balsamic vinegar

Prepare the bread dough (pg 158) and leave it to rise.

CARAMELISED ONIONS: Stir-fry the onions in the olive oil until soft, add the brown sugar and stir-fry until slightly caramelised. Add the vinegar and simmer for 1–2 minutes, or until fragrant.

Preheat the oven to 190 °C. Flatten the dough on a greased baking sheet. Spoon half the onion mixture on top and sprinkle with half the cheese. Fold the dough over the mixture and flatten again. Sprinkle the remaining onions and cheese on top and leave to rise until double in volume. Bake in the preheated oven for 45–60 minutes, or until done. Cover with aluminium foil if the topping is browning too rapidly. *[pg 161]*

SERVES 6–8.

Olive flat bread

1 x basic bread dough (pg 158)
2 onions, chopped
2 cloves garlic, crushed
60 ml olive oil
125 ml pitted and chopped black
    olives
50–75 g feta cheese, crumbled
    (optional)
sprigs of rosemary
50 ml chopped fresh herbs
sea salt flakes for sprinkling on top

Prepare the basic bread dough (pg 158) and leave to rise. Preheat the oven to 190 °C.

Sauté the onions and garlic in the olive oil until soft. Add the olives and cheese. Knock down the dough and knead in the onion and cheese mixture. Flatten the dough on a greased baking sheet, insert sprigs of rosemary and scatter the herbs and sea salt flakes on top. Leave to rise until double in volume and bake in a preheated oven for 40–60 minutes, or until done. Serve with olive oil.

SERVES 6–8.

Flat ash bread

750 ml brown bread flour
250 ml white bread flour
1 sachet (10 g) instant yeast
2 ml salt
60 ml softened lard or butter
500 ml buttermilk

Combine the dry ingredients and, using your fingertips, rub in the lard or butter. Add the buttermilk and mix well. Grease a large sheet of heavy-duty aluminium foil with butter or margarine and put the dough on top. Shape it into an oval about 3 mm thick. Wrap the dough loosely but firmly in the aluminium foil and leave it to rise. Place on top of half-burnt-out coals and cover with more coals. Bake for 30–45 minutes, or until done. Serve with butter.

SERVES 6.

cheese and onion flat bread

'Interesting salads and vegetable dishes can turn an ordinary braai into something extraordinary. At home we usually braai all the meat over the coals and make the side dishes in the kitchen.'

healthy
Salads & vegetables

Salads are a must with a braai. Here are loads to choose from, whether you want to make a simple green salad or something a bit more substantial such as a couscous, rice or pasta salad. Veggies also have their place at a braai, from baked potatoes, char-grilled vegetables, *pap* and pumpkin pie to upside-down vegetable tart and savoury cheesecake. When camping we always have loads of fresh veggies, peeled, whole or wrapped in aluminium foil, to put on the fire.

SALAD DRESSINGS

Basic vinaigrette

I've tweaked this recipe over the years and now I'm never without it. Make loads and keep it in the fridge. It's excellent with salad but the mixture can also be used to marinate fish, prawns or chicken for extra flavour. Also use it to marinate fillet before braaiing – delicious!

30 ml balsamic or red wine vinegar
75 ml oil (mixture of sunflower
   and olive oils)
salt and freshly ground black
   pepper to taste
pinch sugar

Blend all the ingredients with a whisk and drizzle over the salad as needed.

MAKES 100 ML.

VARIATION: Substitute fresh lemon juice for all or some of the vinegar. Add grated lemon zest and 5 ml soy sauce instead of salt. Add 1 crushed clove garlic and 15 ml chopped fresh parsley. Increase the sugar if you prefer a sweeter dressing.

Herb vinaigrette

30 ml balsamic, grape or
   red wine vinegar
75 ml oil (mixture of olive and
   sunflower oils)
45 ml chopped fresh herbs
   such as parsley, oregano,
   basil, thyme or chives
1–2 cloves garlic, crushed (optional)
salt and freshly ground black
   pepper to taste

Blend all the ingredients with a whisk and drizzle over the salad as needed, or serve separately.

MAKES 100 ML.

VARIATION: Add a pinch ground cumin or smoked paprika to the salad dressing.

Mustard vinaigrette

80 ml sunflower or olive oil
30–45 ml fresh lemon juice or grape
   or balsamic vinegar
2–3 cloves garlic, crushed
5–15 ml honey or sugar
5–15 ml wholegrain or Dijon mustard
5–15 ml orange juice concentrate
   (optional)

Blend all the ingredients with a whisk. Chill and use as needed.

MAKES 110 ML.

VARIATION: Flavoured vinegar, such as raspberry vinegar, imparts a special taste to the salad dressing (omit the orange juice concentrate if using). Substitute half the oil with fragrant oil such as walnut or even avocado oil. If desired, add 125 ml chopped fresh strawberries or raspberries and blend in the food processor until smooth.

Africa salad dressing

Blend all the ingredients with a whisk and leave so the flavour can develop.

MAKES 115 ML.

VARIATION 1: Use 7 ml curry powder instead of the spices.

VARIATION 2: Use orange juice instead of lemon juice or vinegar.

TIP: For a creamier variation, add 15–30 ml mayonnaise or plain yoghurt.

80 ml sunflower oil
30–45 ml lemon juice
5 ml paprika (smoked if desired)
5 ml ground cumin
2 ml ground coriander
1 ml ground cinnamon
3–5 ml honey or brown sugar
salt and freshly ground black
  pepper to taste
5 ml grated lemon zest (optional)
45 ml chopped fresh parsley,
  coriander and/or mint

Eastern salad dressing

Blend all the ingredients and use as needed.

MAKES 110 ML.

VARIATION: Use fish or oyster sauce instead of the soy sauce. Add toasted sesame seeds (tip, pg 175) or mustard seeds to the dressing.

60 ml olive or cooking oil
60 ml rice wine vinegar
juice and zest of 2 lemons or limes
15 ml soy sauce
5–10 ml fish or oyster sauce
10–15 ml sesame oil
15 ml sugar
25 ml water
5–10 ml finely grated fresh ginger
2 cloves garlic, crushed
1 chilli, seeded and finely chopped
30 ml chopped fresh coriander
15 ml chopped fresh mint

Mediterranean salad dressing

Blend the salad dressing ingredients in a food processor until smooth.

MAKES 110 ML.

TIP: Spoon this dressing, which is basically a salsa verde, over roasted vegetables (pg 178) as soon as they come off the fire.

30 ml grape vinegar
15 ml lemon juice
30 ml grated Parmesan cheese
80 ml chopped fresh parsley
15 ml chopped fresh mint (optional)
1–2 anchovies, chopped
1 clove garlic, crushed
15 ml capers
5 ml Dijon mustard
180 ml olive oil
30 ml plain yoghurt

Mayonnaise and yoghurt salad dressing

I love mayonnaise but it must be a good quality one. I prefer Hellman's or Kraft – if you buy the low-fat variety you don't have to feel too guilty about this indulgence. Use this dressing for salads, to marinate fish or for spooning over potatoes or vegetables before putting them in the oven.

100 ml good quality mayonnaise
150 ml plain yoghurt
juice and grated zest of 1 orange
    (optional)
5 ml honey or sugar
salt and freshly ground black
    pepper to taste

Whisk together the mayonnaise, yoghurt, orange juice, zest and honey until well blended. Season with salt and pepper and use as needed.

MAKES 250 ML.

VARIATION 1: For extra flavour, add about 15 ml wholegrain mustard, 15 ml curry powder and 1 ml each ground cumin and ground coriander.

VARIATION 2: Omit the orange juice, zest and honey and add a little basil or sun-dried tomato pesto, chermoula (a North African spread) or harissa. Delicious in potato salad or with mushrooms.

SALADS

Green salad with toasted seeds

I tasted this salad at Melissa van Hoogstraten's. Like me, she always keeps a tin of toasted seeds on hand – they add instant flavour and crunch to a green salad and make a delicious snack. The vinaigrette, made with raspberry vinegar, makes a refreshing change to one made with balsamic vinegar.

selection young salad greens
    (rocket, baby spinach and mizuna
    are a good combination)
mustard vinaigrette, made with
    raspberry or red wine vinegar
    (pg 164)
Parmesan cheese shavings
handful or two toasted seed
    mixture, made with sesame,
    sunflower, pumpkin and soy
    seeds (tip, pg 175)

Mix the salad greens and drizzle with the salad dressing. Scatter Parmesan cheese shavings and toasted seeds on top. *[pg 167]*

SERVES 4.

VARIATION 1: Instead of the seeds add a generous handful of pecan or mixed nuts, finely sliced dried fruit (pears are especially good) and coarsely crumbled feta cheese.

VARIATION 2– AVOCADO DRESSING: Mix 1 mashed ripe avocado with 175 ml plain yoghurt and 200 ml basic vinaigrette and drizzle over the salad instead of the mustard vinaigrette. Add cucumber to the salad and scatter with chopped fried bacon instead of the seeds.

VARIATION 3: Roast parboiled sweet potatoes wedges over the coals until golden. Remove from the fire, pour over some of the dressing and leave to cool.

VARIATION 4: Add fresh strawberries and fried crispy bacon.

Mediterranean salad

Put all the salad ingredients except the basil into a salad bowl, preferably a wooden one, and moisten with the salad dressing. Arrange the basil in between.

SERVES 6–8.

VARIATION: Boil baby potatoes until soft, brush with oil and roast rapidly over the fire until crisp. Add to the salad.

TIP: Brush the pepper with oil. Roast over hot coals for about 15 minutes, turning constantly until the skin is charred and shrivelled in parts. Put the pepper in a plastic bag to sweat, and then leave to cool. Remove the skin, halve the pepper and remove the seeds. Cut the pepper into pieces.

1 packet mixed lettuce leaves

500 ml croûtons (fried bread cubes)

1 roasted red pepper, peeled, seeded and cubed (see tip)

1 container (125 g) baby corn, cut into pieces (optional)

1 bunch spring onions, roughly chopped

a few black olives

125 g small Roma tomatoes, halved and/or 3–4 sun-dried tomatoes in vinaigrette, chopped

feta cheese, broken into pieces, or Parmesan cheese shavings

Mediterranean salad dressing (pg 165)

fresh basil to garnish

Beetroot salad

I love beetroot and eat loads of it as is, provided it's young and not big and stringy. Roasting beetroot makes it even more flavoursome. Wrap the beetroot and pickling onions in aluminium foil and roast over the coals.

6 young beetroot, scrubbed and
    halved (do not peel)
6 pickling onions, peeled
    and halved
olive oil
15 ml balsamic vinegar
15 ml brown sugar
30 ml chopped walnuts
mustard vinaigrette (pg 164)
1 green apple, thinly sliced
    (optional)
125 g crumbled blue cheese or
    Cheddar cheese cubes (optional)

Arrange the beetroot and pickling onions, cut side up, each on a sheet of heavy-duty aluminium foil that's been folded in half. Drizzle the olive oil and balsamic vinegar over the pickling onions and sprinkle with the brown sugar. Wrap tightly in the aluminium foil and roast over the coals until done – it will take about 1 hour. Remove the aluminium foil, cool slightly and peel the beetroot. Mix the walnuts with the vinaigrette and add to the hot vegetables. Leave to cool and add the apple and blue or Cheddar cheese if using.

SERVES 6.

Broccoli salad

One of décor fundi Marcia Margolius' great standbys.

SALAD
1 head broccoli, broken into florets
1 packet (200 g) cherry tomatoes,
    halved
2 red onions, halved and
    thinly sliced
25 ml poppy seeds
60 ml sunflower seeds, toasted

SALAD DRESSING
45 ml finely chopped onion
125 ml sugar
125 ml white vinegar
250 ml sunflower oil
5 ml salt
10 ml Dijon mustard

Mix the salad ingredients. Blend the salad dressing ingredients and drizzle over the salad. Leave to marinate in the fridge for at least 8 hours before serving. *[pg 168]*

SERVES 6–8.

Sweet 'n sour cucumber salad

This salad goes particularly well with spicy dishes such as Cajun chicken (pg 114) or curry.

Halve the cucumber lengthways, then halve again. Remove the seeds and slice the cucumber into long strips using a potato peeler. Drizzle the salad dressing over the cucumber and leave to stand for 1 hour. Sprinkle coriander and peanuts on top just before serving.

SERVES 4.

1 English cucumber
Eastern salad dressing (pg 165)
a large handful fresh coriander,
   well rinsed
peanuts

Red cabbage and apple salad

Mix together finely chopped red cabbage and thin slivers of Granny Smith apples. Drizzle with mustard vinaigrette (pg 164) and sprinkle with coriander leaves and mixed nuts.

VARIATION: Add 125 g crumbled blue cheese or cubes of matured Cheddar cheese to the salad.

Avocado and orange salad

I came across this delicious salad on a trip to the Lowveld. Avocado and orange are perfect together; but you can also add blue cheese for extra flavour.

Arrange the salad leaves on a platter and top with the avocado, bananas (or apples or pineapple) and oranges. Sprinkle with walnuts and coriander leaves and drizzle with the salad dressing. *[pg 171]*

SERVES 3–4.

VARIATION: Add blue cheese to the salad and use mayonnaise and yoghurt salad dressing (pg 166) instead of the Africa salad dressing. Use mint instead of coriander.

mix of 4 types of salad leaves, such
   as rocket, mizuna, watercress
   and endive
2 avocados, peeled, pip removed,
   and sliced
3 bananas, 2 Granny Smith apples
   or 1 pineapple, peeled and sliced
2 oranges, peeled and segmented
125 ml walnuts or pecan nuts,
   chopped
fresh coriander or mint leaves to
   garnish (optional)
Africa salad dressing, variation 2
   (pg 165)

American potato salad

Gherkins, hard-boiled eggs and olives are delicious in potato salad.

1 kg baby potatoes
45 ml apple cider vinegar
90 ml mayonnaise
90 ml plain yoghurt
30 ml Dijon mustard
1 medium onion, finely chopped
4 gherkins, finely chopped
black olives, pitted and chopped
salt and freshly ground black
   pepper to taste
2–3 hard-boiled eggs
100 ml chopped fried bacon
   (optional)
chopped fresh parsley

Cook the potatoes in boiling salted water until soft. Drain and remove the skins if desired. Pour the vinegar over the potatoes while still warm. Mix the mayonnaise, yoghurt and mustard and add the onion, gherkins and olives. Season with salt and pepper and mix with the potatoes. Chop the egg yolks and whites separately and scatter over the salad along with the chopped bacon if using. Scatter parsley over the top.

SERVES 6.

VARIATION 1: Add feta cheese to the salad.

VARIATION 2: Make a rice salad by substituting 750 ml cooked brown rice for the potatoes.

TIP: Fry 30 ml fresh breadcrumbs in melted butter until crisp. Add the chopped parsley, mix with the egg yolks and whites and scatter over the salad.

Curried potato salad

500 g potatoes
50 ml apple cider vinegar
salt and freshly ground black
   pepper to taste
1 onion, chopped
cooking oil for frying
15 ml mild curry powder
250 ml mayonnaise
125 ml plain yoghurt
15 ml lemon juice
2 apples, cored and cubed or sliced
   (do not peel)
2 stalks celery, thinly sliced
100 ml chopped fried bacon

Boil the potatoes in their jackets in salted water until done. Drain, rinse under cold water and remove the skins. Cube or slice the potatoes and sprinkle with the vinegar, salt and pepper. Leave to cool. Sauté the onion in a little oil until soft, add the curry powder and stir-fry for about 1 minute or until fragrant. Leave to cool and mix with the mayonnaise, yoghurt and lemon juice. Mix with the potatoes and add the apples and celery. Scatter the bacon on top and chill until ready to serve.

SERVES 6.

TIP: See variation for Mediterranean salad (pg 167) for another delicious potato salad.

Apple and celery are added to this potato salad with its fragrant curry-flavoured salad dressing.

Sweet melon salad

Sweet melon is a favourite fruit salad ingredient but it also combines beautifully with savoury ingredients such as ham and cheese. This is a wonderfully refreshing summer salad.

Arrange the sweet melon and avocado on a large salad platter. Scatter the cheese and bacon on top and pour over the vinaigrette. Scatter the greens on top. *[pg 59]*

SERVES 4.

VARIATION 1: Nectarine or fresh mango slices also go well in this salad.

VARIATION 2: Omit the bacon and combine the fruit with blue cheese. Then moisten with Eastern salad dressing (pg 165).

TIP: If rocket is unobtainable make a bed of shredded endive or iceberg lettuce and pile the rest of the ingredients on top.

TIP: Use fresh mozzarella balls (bocconcini) instead of the feta cheese.

1 sweet melon, peeled and sliced
   or cubed
2 ripe avocados, peeled, stones
   removed and sliced
3 rounds feta cheese with pepper,
   coarsely crumbled
125 g back bacon, fried and
   chopped
mustard vinaigrette (pg 164)
1 packet fresh rocket or mizuna

Chickpea and butternut salad

Butternut and chickpeas go well together, especially when moistened with Africa salad dressing. Make the salad go further by adding couscous (see variation).

3 kg butternut, peeled and cubed

45 ml olive oil

5–10 ml ground cumin

salt flakes

Africa salad dressing (pg 165)

2 cans (400 g each) chickpeas, drained

2 handfuls rocket

chopped spring onions, coriander and parsley to sprinkle on top

Preheat the oven to 200 °C. Arrange the butternut cubes in a single layer on a baking sheet and drizzle with the oil. Season with the cumin and salt flakes. Roast until done. Pour over half the salad dressing and leave to cool. Then add the chickpeas and remaining salad dressing. Arrange the rocket on a salad platter and top with the salad. Scatter the spring onions and herbs on top.

SERVES 6.

TIP: Substitute a can of butter beans for 1 can of chickpeas.

TIP: Roast the butternut over the fire. First boil or steam it until three-quarters done and still firm. Arrange in a single layer in a hinged braai grid and drizzle with the oil. Season with the cumin and salt and roast over hot coals for about 15 minutes, or until done and crisp.

VARIATION – COUSCOUS SALAD: Pour 250 ml boiling vegetable stock over 250 ml couscous, leave until swollen and fluff with a fork. Spoon the butternut salad on top and mix lightly. Add a handful of sultanas and/or chopped dried apricots if desired and scatter almond flakes on top.

Quick chickpea salads

(1) Cut 500 g scraped carrots into julienne strips. Add a handful of raisins, toasted sesame seeds and 1 can (400 g) chickpeas. Moisten with Africa salad dressing (pg 165).

(2) Mix 1 can (400 g) chickpeas with halved cherry tomatoes, cucumber and avocado slices and feta cheese. Mix 125 ml buttermilk with 30 ml snipped chives, 5 ml honey and 15 ml wholegrain mustard and pour over the salad. Sprinkle with toasted sesame seeds (tip, pg 175). *[pg 60]*

SERVES 6.

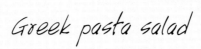
Greek pasta salad

Mediterranean couscous salad

250 ml boiling vegetable stock
250 ml couscous
herb vinaigrette (pg 164) or
    Mediterranean dressing (pg 165)
5 ml sea salt flakes
200 g cherry tomatoes, halved,
    or 6 sun-dried tomatoes in
    vinaigrette, chopped
1 avocado, peeled and sliced
4 rounds feta cheese
100 ml black olives, pitted

Pour the vegetable stock over the couscous and leave until swollen. Flake with a fork and add half the herb vinaigrette or Mediterranean dressing. Mix the couscous with the remaining ingredients and pour over the remaining vinaigrette or dressing. Serve with toasted ciabatta bread if desired.

SERVES 6–8.

VARIATION 1: Add a variety of char-grilled vegetables (pg 178) to the mixture. Add more herb vinaigrette, having soaked the vegetables in the dressing beforehand.

VARIATION 2: Add 1 can (400 g) chickpeas or butter beans to the couscous.

Crushed wheat salad

This salad is a variation of tabbouleh, the well-known Middle-Eastern salad made with bulgur wheat.

200 g crushed wheat, soaked
    in water
vegetable stock powder (quantity
    as per instructions on tin)
75 ml lemon juice
100 ml olive oil
5–10 ml sun-dried tomato pesto
    (optional)
125 ml chopped fresh parsley
45 ml chopped fresh mint
5 spring onions, roughly chopped
4 Roma or plum tomatoes, chopped
¼ English cucumber, diced
salt and freshly ground black
    pepper to taste

Drain the soaked wheat and boil in fresh water until just soft. Add the vegetable stock powder towards the end of the cooking time. Mix the lemon juice, olive oil and tomato pesto, if using, and add to the wheat. Add the remaining salad ingredients and mix.

SERVES 8–10.

VARIATION: Chop roasted brinjal slices and add to the salad.

Marinated vegetable and bean salad

Roast vegetables such as peppers, brinjals, baby marrows and onions over the coals or in the oven until soft and lightly browned. Remove the skins of the peppers if desired. Fry 2 cloves garlic in 15 ml oil until soft, add 2 cans (65 g each) tomato paste, 200 ml brown vinegar, 100 ml brown sugar, 10 ml prepared mustard and 5 ml salt. Boil for 5 minutes, add the vegetables and 2 cans (400 g each) drained chickpeas and bring to the boil. Spoon into sterilised jars and seal while hot. Leave for a day or two to allow flavours to develop. This salad will last in the fridge for up to 3 weeks after opening.

Brown rice salad

This salad is packed with nuts, seeds and other treats. Make it two days in advance so the flavours can blend and develop.

Boil the brown rice in salted water until done. Stir-fry the leeks and garlic in the oil until soft and add to the rice along with the remaining ingredients. Chill for at least 12–24 hours so the flavours can develop. *[pg 107]*

SERVES 8–10.

VARIATION: Grill slices of halloumi cheese over the coals. Cut into smaller pieces and add to the salad.

TIP: Toast seeds and nuts in a dry pan until lightly browned. Shake the pan continuously to prevent burning.

500 ml brown rice
1 packet young leeks, sliced into thin rings
3 cloves garlic, crushed
olive oil
250 ml toasted cashew or pecan nuts
125 ml mixture of toasted seeds, such as pine kernels and pumpkin and sunflower seeds
250 ml sultanas
1 bunch spring onions, chopped
250 ml chopped fresh parsley or coriander
2 x mustard vinaigrette (variation, pg 164)

Greek pasta salad

Pasta salad is an evergreen. Instead of mayonnaise I've moistened the pasta with a herby salad dressing. If you prefer a creamier result use mayonnaise blended with a little pesto (see tip).

Cook the pasta in rapidly boiling salted water until just soft. Drain and moisten with the vinaigrette while still hot. Add the remaining ingredients, except the greens and parsley. Chill well. Arrange the greens on a platter, spoon the pasta salad on top and garnish with parsley. *[pg 173]*

SERVES 4–6.

VARIATION: For added creaminess blend a little basil or sun-dried tomato pesto with mayonnaise or plain yoghurt and mix with the salad instead of the dressing.

TIP – QUICK PASTA SALAD: Mix leftover pasta with any ready-made salad dressing while the pasta is still warm. Add chopped sun-dried tomatoes and ham and serve on a bed of lettuce. Scatter Parmesan cheese shavings on top.

250 g penne pasta or macaroni
herb vinaigrette (variation with smoked paprika, pg 164)
3 fingers Danish feta or goat cheese, roughly crumbled
2 spring onions, chopped
1 red pepper, roasted, seeded and cut into pieces (optional)
200 g cherry tomatoes, halved
20 black olives, pitted
125 g back bacon, fried and chopped, or 4 frankfurters or Russian sausages, sliced and fried
rocket or mizuna to serve (optional)
Italian parsley to garnish

Eastern noodle salad

Eastern noodle salad

The exotic flavours of the East have become increasingly popular. Try giving a pasta salad, made with ribbon pasta or Chinese noodles, an Eastern twist for a change.

SALAD: Cook the pasta or noodles in rapidly boiling salted water until just soft, and drain. Immediately add the sesame oil and soy sauce. Leave to cool and add the remaining salad ingredients.

SALAD DRESSING: Bring the salad dressing ingredients to the boil in a small saucepan just before serving. Simmer until creamy. Cool slightly before transferring to a jug and serving lukewarm with the salad. Serve immediately. *[pg 176]*

SERVES 4–6.

VARIATION 1: Substitute Eastern salad dressing (pg 165) for the salad dressing.

VARIATION 2: Roast red peppers, portabellini mushrooms and baby marrows over the coals and use instead of the fresh vegetables. Also add 12 peeled and stir-fried prawns if desired.

TIP: Use 2 packets instant noodles if desired.

SALAD

250 g thin ribbon pasta or
   Chinese noodles
15 ml sesame oil
15 m soy sauce
freshly ground black pepper
   to taste
½ English cucumber, cut into
   short, thin strips
2 carrots, peeled and julienned
6 baby corn, cut into smaller pieces
2 spring onions, chopped

SALAD DRESSING

300 ml water
1 clove garlic, crushed
15 ml soy sauce
5–10 ml sweet chilli sauce
45–60 ml crunchy peanut butter
5 ml ground cumin
5 ml ground coriander
15 ml rice wine vinegar or
   lemon juice
2 ml sugar

African bean salad

This salad is excellent wrapped in tortillas and served with kebabs. The salad will keep in the fridge for up to a week.

Drain the beans, chickpeas and corn and pour over the salad dressing. Mix together. Scatter the coriander on top.

SERVES 4–6.

1 can (410 g) red kidney beans
1 can (410 g) butter beans
1 can (400 g) chickpeas
1 can (400 g) whole kernel corn
Africa salad dressing (add
   yoghurt for extra creaminess,
   see tip, pg 165)
large handful fresh coriander

VEGETABLES ON THE BRAAI

Interesting veggies and side dishes can turn an ordinary braai of chops and sausage into a memorable feast. Don't neglect these deliciously nourishing dishes – ensure there are plenty of them on the table.

char-grilled vegetables

Char-grilled vegetables are all the rage at the moment so keep plenty of peppers, baby marrows, brinjals, onions and mushrooms on hand when braaiing – they're ready in minutes when done over the coals. When it comes to butternut and sweet potatoes, they're best cut into chunks or slices and parboiled before putting them on the fire otherwise they'll take ages to cook. You can also put halloumi cheese on the fire – it's one of the few cheeses that retain its shape when heated. Serve with vegetables instead of feta.

red and yellow peppers, seeded
    and cut into wide strips
baby marrows, cut into thick slices
1 bunch spring onions, roughly
    chopped
brinjals, sliced lengthways
large brown mushrooms,
    cut into thick slices
herb vinaigrette (pg 164) or Africa
    salad dressing (pg 165) or
    Mediterranean dressing (pg 165)
sea salt flakes
feta cheese or 1 packet halloumi
    cheese, sliced (optional,
    but preferable with the herb
    vinaigrette)
olive oil

Put all the vegetables in a dish and pour over one of the salad dressings. Leave to stand for at least 2 hours. Remove the vegetables from the salad dressing (reserve the dressing) and arrange in a hinged braai grid or on an open grid. Sprinkle with salt and grill over hot coals for 4–5 minutes, or until seared. Baste with the vinaigrette from time to time. Sprinkle with feta if preferred, otherwise arrange the halloumi cheese slices on the grid, brush with oil and braai rapidly or until lightly seared. Turn the cheese once and serve immediately with the vegetables.

VARIATION: Add butternut and sweet potatoes if making the vegetables with the Africa salad dressing. Peel the butternut and scrub the sweet potatoes and cut both vegetables into thick slices. Parboil until just beginning to soften.

TIP: If using the herb vinaigrette, spoon the char-grilled vegetables into pita breads that have been lightly toasted on the fire. You can also toast slices of ciabatta or farm loaf over the coals or serve the vegetables with griddlecakes. Before piling the vegetables on the bread you can first stack it with lettuce leaves. You can also mix cream cheese or smooth cottage cheese with a spoonful or two of basil or sun-dried tomato pesto and serve it with the vegetables and bread.

TIP: These char-grilled vegetables can be added to Mediterranean couscous salad (pg 174).

Potatoes and sweet potatoes

Prick the skins of whole potatoes and sweet potatoes and brush with butter or oil. Sprinkle with sea salt flakes and wrap in a few layers of aluminium foil. Braai over medium coals for about 1 hour, or until soft and done. Turn from time to time. You can also bury the vegetables in burnt-out coals and leave them to bake.

TIP: When baking potatoes in the oven at 200 °C don't wrap them in aluminium foil – simply put them on the oven rack.

Stuffings

Cut a deep cross in the potatoes or sweet potatoes and squeeze them to open. Prepare the stuffing and spoon inside the potato.

STUFFING 1: Mix whole kernel corn with chopped fried bacon and chives and add 125 ml crumbly cottage cheese and 60 ml sour cream (or 250 g cream cheese, creamed cottage cheese or crème fraîche). Spoon into baked potatoes.

STUFFING 2: Roughly chop vegetables such as mushrooms and red peppers and stir-fry with a chopped onion, garlic clove and rosemary until fragrant. Add a generous dash of soy sauce. Mix with cottage cheese and sour cream and spoon into baked potatoes.

STUFFING 3: Mix 50 g blue cheese with crumbly cottage cheese and/or sour cream. Spoon into baked potatoes or sweet potatoes.

STUFFING 4: Mix about 100 g butter with the zest of 1 orange, 60 ml chopped fresh coriander leaves and 1 crushed clove garlic. Spoon into baked sweet potatoes and sprinkle with ground cinnamon, if preferred.

Roasted garlic bulbs

Brush a whole garlic bulb with oil and wrap in aluminium foil. Roast over the coals for about 40 minutes, or until done. Leave to cool before squeezing out the garlic purée. Mix with mayonnaise and serve with baked potatoes or potato wedges or spread the purée on bread. *[pg 181]*

Whole mealies

If the mealies still have their leaves intact do not remove them – simply pull them back, taking care not to break them off. Spread butter (flavoured with garlic or chillies and fresh coriander if desired) over the mealies and fold back the leaves. Secure with string near the tip. Arrange the mealies on the grid and roast until done. If the leaves have already been removed wrap the mealies in aluminium foil. *[pg 179]*

Roasted brinjals

2 large or 4 small brinjals
salt and freshly ground black
  pepper to taste
olive oil
lemon juice

STUFFING
1 onion, chopped
4 cloves garlic, crushed
olive oil
4–6 Roma or plum tomatoes,
  peeled and seeded
15 ml sun-dried tomato pesto
salt, ground black pepper and
  sugar to taste
black olives, pitted (optional)
capers (optional)
feta or ricotta cheese (optional)

Prick the whole brinjals all over and braai over medium coals for at least 20 minutes, or until blackened on the outside and soft inside. Cut a cross in the top of each brinjal and squeeze to open. Season with salt and pepper and drizzle generously with olive oil. Sprinkle with a little lemon juice.

STUFFING: While the brinjals are on the braai, fry the onion and garlic in a little oil until soft. Add the tomatoes and stir-fry until fragrant. Add the tomato pesto and season with salt, pepper and a little sugar. Add a few olives and capers if using. Spoon the filling into the cooked brinjals. Serve with toasted slices of ciabatta bread and crumble feta or ricotta cheese on top if desired. *[pg 181]*

SERVES 4.

TIP: Grill slices of halloumi cheese over the coals and stuff inside the brinjals. Serve with chimichurri (pg 14) or coriander pesto (pg 14).

Roasted peppers

These peppers are especially good with Italian leg of pork.

6 whole red or yellow peppers
150 ml olive oil
3 cloves garlic, crushed
1 tin or jar (50 g) anchovies
  (optional)
160 ml white wine
45 ml chopped fresh parsley

Brush the outside of the whole peppers with oil and put on the grid over medium coals. Roast for at least 20 minutes, or until the skins begin to blacken and shrivel and the flesh is soft. Put the peppers in a plastic bag, tie the bag and leave the peppers to sweat until cooled. Remove the skins and seeds and cut the peppers into pieces or strips. Meanwhile, heat the 150 ml olive oil in a pan and sauté the garlic until soft. Add the anchovies, if using, and the white wine and parsley. Simmer for 5 minutes and pour over the peppers. Leave to cool. Serve with Italian leg of pork (pg 66). *[pg 181]*

SERVES 6–8.

STUFFED VEGETABLES

Butternut with spinach or mealie stuffing

Halve an unpeeled butternut and remove the seeds. Stuff the hollows with shredded spinach mixed with a generous quantity of cream, ricotta or feta cheese, pitted olives and sun-dried tomatoes. Or mix whole kernel corn with cream or ricotta cheese, a few finely sliced piquant peppers and chopped, fried bacon. Wrap the stuffed butternut in aluminium foil and roast over medium coals for about 1 hour until soft and cooked.

Peppers with couscous stuffing

Peppers make a perfect receptacle for fillings. Halve the peppers, remove the seeds and white membranes and brush with oil on the outside. Stuff the pepper halves with cooked couscous mixed with pitted olives, chopped cherry tomatoes and pine nuts. Cover the stuffing with a slice of cheese, such as mozzarella or another soft cheese, and roast over medium coals until seared on the outside and the filling is heated through. Drizzle with a little herb vinaigrette (pg 164) just before serving.

Mushrooms with cheese filling

Wipe the outside of 5 large brown mushrooms and brush with oil. Mix 5–10 ml basil or sun-dried tomato pesto with ricotta cheese and moisten with a spoonful of mayonnaise. Fill the mushroom hollows with the mixture. Sprinkle with grated Parmesan cheese and grill over the coals until brown on the outside and the filling is heated through. Delicious cooked in a kettle braai or on a gas braai with a dome lid.

VARIATION: Spoon a little pesto – try coriander or almond pesto for a change – in the mushroom hollows and top with a slice of Camembert cheese. Grill until hot and the cheese has melted slightly.

Vegetable parcels

Cut a variety of vegetables into bite-sized pieces and divide among a few sheets of aluminium foil. Make a selection of flavoured butters (pg 34) or mix butter with herbs such as rosemary or thyme, or spices such as cumin or cinnamon. Alternatively, mix the butter with chillies or garlic. Dot the vegetables with the butter, wrap in the aluminium foil sheets and cook over medium coals until done.

TIP: Hazelnut butter is delicious with vegetables. Mix 100 ml butter with 50 g chopped hazelnuts and the zest of ½ lemon. Dot the vegetables with the butter mixture while cooking or serve separately with the cooked vegetables.

SKEWERED VEGETABLES

Potato kebabs

Thread cooked baby potatoes and butternut cubes onto kebab skewers along with pickling onions and large pepper cubes. Brush with easy braai sauce (pg 108) and roast over medium coals until done and brown on the outside. Baste with the braai sauce from time to time. *[pg 182]*

VARIATION 1: Use honey and mustard salad dressing or a ready-made cook-in sauce if you're in a hurry.

VARIATION 2: Wrap each baby potato in a rasher of bacon before threading onto the skewers.

Skewered potato wedges

Boil large potatoes in salted water until soft, cut into wedges and thread onto skewers. Spray with olive oil spray and season with sea salt flakes. Roast over the fire until golden brown. Serve with garlic mayonnaise (ssee roasted garlic bulbs, pg 179) or cream cheese blended with a little pesto.

vegetable and cheese kebabs

Thread small Roma tomatoes, portabellini mushrooms, rolled-up spinach leaves and fairly large cubes of halloumi cheese onto skewers. Roast over the fire until brown and the cheese has melted. Mix a little chopped garlic and chilli flakes with olive oil and baste the kebabs with the mixture while roasting.

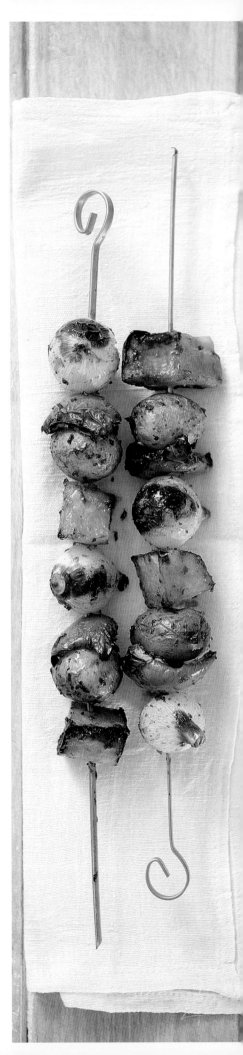

VEGETABLE POTJIES

Africa vegetable pot

Green bananas, butternut and sweet potatoes cooked in a fragrant coconut milk sauce. Delicious!

Heat the oil in a potjie or heavy-based saucepan and fry the onions and garlic until soft. Add the spices and stir-fry for about 1 minute, or until fragrant. Add the butternut, sweet potatoes, red pepper and chillies and stir-fry until coated with the spices. Add the bananas, tomatoes, corn and coconut milk, and scatter the thyme and oregano on top. Pour over the orange juice and season with salt and pepper. Bring to the boil, reduce the heat and simmer over low heat for about 45 minutes, or until the vegetables are soft. Scatter with coriander leaves and serve with basmati rice and sambals (see tip).

SERVES 8.

TIP: Serve with sambals such as chopped tomato and onion, coconut and chopped cucumber and chilli.

30 ml cooking oil

3 onions, finely chopped

4 cloves garlic, finely chopped

30 ml ground coriander

2 ml ground nutmeg

5 ml ground cumin

500 ml peeled butternut cubes

2 sweet potatoes, scrubbed and sliced

1 red pepper, seeded and cut into
   large pieces

2–4 chillies, seeded and chopped

2–3 green bananas, cut into thick slices

1 can (400 g) whole peeled tomatoes

1 can (400 g) whole kernel corn, drained

1 can (400 g) coconut milk

5 ml chopped fresh thyme

10 ml chopped fresh oregano

125 ml orange juice

salt and freshly ground black pepper
   to taste

15 ml chopped fresh coriander

Tomato-vegetable pot

Heat the oil in a potjie and sauté the onion and garlic until soft. Add the brinjal and sauté until soft. Add more oil if necessary. Add the red pepper and baby marrows and sauté until soft and done. Add the tomatoes and sprinkle the herbs and sugar on top. Simmer for about 7 minutes, or until fragrant. Season well with salt and pepper and serve with *krummelpap* or couscous.

SERVES 4–6.

olive oil

1 onion, sliced into rings

3 cloves garlic, crushed

1 medium unpeeled brinjal, diced

1 red pepper, seeded and diced

4 baby marrows, sliced

1–2 cans (400 g each) chopped
   tomatoes

15 ml chopped fresh herbs such as
   oregano, thyme and basil

pinch sugar

salt and freshly ground black
   pepper to taste

Mayonnaise potatoes

VEGETABLE SIDE DISHES

Mayonnaise potatoes

A baked potato dish is always a winner with braaivleis. I often make this version when we decide to have a braai on the spur of the moment. It's quick, easy and requires very little effort. I prefer to boil the potatoes until soft before putting them in the oven.

Preheat the oven to 180 °C. Layer the potatoes and onion (if using) in a greased ovenproof dish. Mix the mayonnaise (or mayonnaise mixture) and mustard or pesto, spoon over the potatoes and onion and top with a generous scattering of feta or Parmesan cheese. Bake for about 30 minutes, or until brown. *[pg 184]*

SERVES 6–8.

TIP: Make concertina potatoes by slicing the whole potatoes, but do not cut all the way through. Proceed as above.

VARIATION 1: Use cream instead of mayonnaise and omit the mustard or pesto. Season well with salt and pepper and thyme. Add a can or jar of anchovies with their oil if desired.

VARIATION 2: Cut the potato into slices, layer them and season well with salt and pepper. Scatter 125 ml marinated sun-dried tomatoes and 2 crushed cloves garlic on top and pour over 250 ml white wine. Sprinkle with Parmesan cheese and bake for about 40 minutes, or until done.

8 large potatoes, boiled until soft
   and cut into wedges
1 onion, sliced (optional)
300 ml good quality mayonnaise, or
   substitute milk or plain yoghurt
   for 100 ml of the mayonnaise
30 ml prepared mustard or basil or
   sun-dried tomato pesto
feta or 125 ml grated Parmesan
   cheese to sprinkle on top

Delicious mashed potatoes

Herb-infused milk adds a special flavour to mashed potatoes. Especially good with Langebaan chermoula fish (pg 136) or steak prepared in a blue cheese marinade.

Boil the potatoes in salted water until soft, then peel them and cut into fairly small pieces. Meanwhile, heat the milk with the garlic and herbs to just below boiling point. Remove from the heat and leave to stand so the flavours of the herbs can infuse the milk. Mash the boiled potatoes. Strain the milk, mix with the olive oil and gradually add to the mashed potatoes, stirring until smooth. Season with salt and pepper and stir in the feta cheese if desired.

SERVES 4.

VARIATION: Use blue cheese instead of feta cheese and pour over a generous quantity of melted butter.

7–8 potatoes
150 ml full-cream milk
2 cloves garlic
1 sprig rosemary
1 sprig thyme
125 ml olive oil
salt and freshly ground black
   pepper to taste
1 round feta cheese, crumbled
   (optional)

Potato cake

Surprise guests with a potato cake baked in a loose-bottomed tin.

1 onion, sliced into rings

2–4 cloves garlic, crushed

olive oil

250 g button, portabellini or brown
    mushrooms, sliced

2 red or yellow peppers, seeded
    and cubed

salt and freshly ground black
    pepper to taste

45 ml chopped fresh herbs such as
    parsley, basil, thyme and chives

125 ml fine fresh breadcrumbs

4 large potatoes, boiled, peeled
    and neatly sliced

300 g mozzarella cheese, sliced

grated Parmesan cheese for
    sprinkling on top

Preheat the oven to 190 °C. Grease a 20 cm loose-bottomed cake tin with non-stick spray. Sauté the onion and garlic in olive oil until soft. Add the mushrooms and peppers and sauté until done. Season with salt, pepper and the herbs. Sprinkle the bottom and sides of the tin with some of the breadcrumbs. Arrange half the potato slices in the bottom of the tin, spoon half the vegetable mixture on top, spreading it evenly, and top with half the mozzarella cheese slices. Repeat the layers and sprinkle the remaining breadcrumbs and a little Parmesan cheese on top. Bake in the preheated oven for 25–30 minutes, or until the cheese has melted and is golden brown. Leave the cake to cool slightly in the tin before carefully removing and transferring it to a serving platter. Serve hot.

SERVES 6.

VARIATION – SKOTTEL BRAAI POTATOES: Stir-fry diced boiled potatoes in the pan of a gas braai or over the coals in a pan, along with the vegetables and a little chopped bacon until cooked and fragrant. Scatter the herbs and crumbled feta cheese on top. Delicious for brunch.

Roasted whole pumpkin

Stuff a whole pumpkin with bread and cheese and bake it in the oven or in a kettle or gas braai.
Serve as is and cut into slices so guests can each have a slice of pumpkin and stuffing. Delicious!

1 whole pumpkin (± 2 kg)

15 ml olive oil

25 ml butter

6 slices wholewheat bread, cubed

15 ml Marmite

450 ml boiling water

2 extra-large eggs

500 ml sour cream

2 ml ground nutmeg

15 ml fresh thyme

15 ml chopped fresh parsley

salt and freshly ground black
    pepper to taste

200 g mozzarella and/or Cheddar
    cheese, grated

Preheat the oven to 190 °C. Spray a large baking sheet with non-stick spray. Cut off the top third of the pumpkin and reserve the 'lid'. Remove the seeds. Heat the oil and butter, fry the bread until crisp and spoon into the pumpkin. Dissolve the Marmite in the boiling water and pour into the pumpkin. Mix the remaining ingredients and spoon into the pumpkin. Cover with the 'lid' and aluminium foil if desired and bake for about 1½ hours, or until the pumpkin flesh is soft. Transfer to a serving platter.

SERVES 8.

vegetable pie with phyllo pastry

I always keep a roll of phyllo pastry in the freezer at our weekend house. This means you don't first have to make pastry if you suddenly decide to bake a tart. Phyllo pastry is also low in fat. For this tart the pastry casing is only filled with vegetables and not a rich custard mixture, which needs plenty of baking time. Sprinkle the tart with feta cheese if desired.

Preheat the oven to 180 °C. Grease a 23 cm ovenproof pie dish with butter or non-stick spray. Brush each sheet of phyllo with melted butter or olive oil. Line the dish with the sheets of phyllo pastry so the pastry hangs over the sides. Drain the sun-dried tomatoes (reserve the vinaigrette) and chop finely. Sauté the garlic, onions, red pepper, mushrooms and baby marrows in a little heated oil until soft. Add half the chopped sun-dried tomatoes and herbs and spoon into the bottom of the dish. Arrange the fresh tomato slices on top, season well with salt and pepper and scatter the olives and feta cheese (if using) on top. Sprinkle with the remaining herbs, sun-dried tomatoes and reserved vinaigrette. Fold the edges of the pastry over the filling and bake in the preheated oven for about 30 minutes, or until the pastry is done, the cheese melted and the filling is heated through. Serve lukewarm.

SERVES 6.

VARIATION: Use shortcrust pastry made in the food processor instead of the phyllo pastry.

TIP: Defrost the phyllo pastry in the fridge and cover with a damp cloth while working with it, otherwise it will dry out.

8–12 phyllo pastry sheets

60 ml melted butter or olive oil spray

1 packet (240 g) sun-dried tomatoes in olive oil vinaigrette

4 cloves garlic, crushed

2 medium onions, peeled and sliced

1 red pepper, seeded and diced (optional)

2 brown mushrooms, sliced (optional)

2 baby marrows, sliced

olive oil

45 ml chopped fresh oregano and/or basil and/or Italian parsley

3 large Roma tomatoes, sliced

salt and freshly ground black pepper to taste

12–14 black olives, pitted

2–4 rounds feta cheese (optional)

Bread tart

Serve this bread tart instead of garlic bread next time you have a braai. Made with slices of toasted French loaf layered with feta cheese and baked in an egg custard, this dish is delicious served with a spoonful of pesto.

1 French loaf, thinly sliced
garlic butter
6 spring onions, roughly chopped
45 ml chopped fresh basil, oregano
    or Italian parsley
100 g feta cheese, crumbled
3 extra-large eggs
200 ml plain yoghurt
200 ml milk or cream
salt and freshly ground black
    pepper to taste
30 ml grated Parmesan cheese

Switch on the oven grill and grease a 24 cm pie dish with butter or non-stick spray. Spread the bread slices on both sides with garlic butter. Arrange them on a baking sheet and toast lightly. Preheat the oven to 170 °C.

Arrange half the bread in the bottom of the prepared pie dish. Scatter the spring onions, herbs and feta cheese on top and arrange the remaining bread slices on top. Beat together the eggs, yoghurt and milk or cream and season generously with salt and pepper. Pour over the ingredients in the dish. Sprinkle with the Parmesan cheese and bake the tart in the preheated oven for about 40 minutes, or until the filling is set and golden brown. Turn out onto a wire rack to cool. Serve with a little sun-dried tomato or basil pesto.

SERVES 4–6.

Savoury cheesecake

You can add spinach to this four-cheeses savoury cheesecake if desired.

CRUST
2 packets (200 g each) cream
    crackers, crushed
4 egg whites, lightly whisked until
    soft peaks form
30 ml poppy seeds (optional)

FILLING
250 g ricotta cheese
250 g creamed cottage cheese
250 g mozzarella or Cheddar
    cheese, grated
4 egg yolks, lightly whisked with
    125 ml milk
1 ml cayenne pepper and/or
    paprika (smoked if desired)
salt and freshly ground black
    pepper to taste
80 ml grated Parmesan cheese

Preheat the oven to 180 °C. Grease a 22 cm loose-bottomed cake tin with butter or non-stick spray.

CRUST: Mix all the crust ingredients well and press onto the bottom and around the sides of the cake tin. Bake for 10 minutes, and then chill until needed.

FILLING: Mix all the filling ingredients except the Parmesan cheese and spoon into the prepared pie crust. Sprinkle the Parmesan cheese on top and bake for about 40 minutes in the preheated oven, or until the filling is firm. Leave in the switched-off oven to cool for 10 minutes before carefully removing from the cake tin. Serve the cheesecake lukewarm.

SERVES 10.

VARIATION – SPINACH CHEESECAKE: Sauté an onion in a little olive oil until soft. Add 300 g spinach and heat until soft. Squeeze out all the liquid and add to the cheese mixture. Season with 1 ml ground nutmeg instead of the cayenne pepper or paprika.

Sweet pumpkin pie

Halve and cook 4–5 butternuts or 500 g pumpkin cubes until soft. Cream together 125 g butter and 125 ml sugar. Whisk in 3–4 eggs, one at a time. Sift 125 ml cake flour and 15 ml baking powder over the mixture and stir in 250 ml milk and the cooked butternut or pumpkin. Spoon into a greased dish and bake at 180 °C for 1 hour, or until the pie is golden brown and firm.

SERVES 6.

Braai pap tart

This tart is a delicious alternative to krummelpap at a braai. Serve with braised tomato and sausage.

Preheat the oven to 180 °C. Grease a 30 cm pie dish. Sprinkle the peanuts in the bottom of the dish.

Add the mealie meal and salt to the water and cook until thick and done. Cool slightly and stir in the corn. Heat the oil and stir-fry the onion and mushrooms until soft. Add the bacon and half the Cheddar cheese. Stir in the cream or cream cheese. Layer the *pap* and vegetable mixture in the pie dish, sprinkle with the remaining cheese and bake in the preheated oven for about 45 minutes, or until done. Serve lukewarm.

SERVES 6.

125 ml chopped peanuts (preferably unsalted)
250 ml mealie meal
salt
1 litre water
1 can (400 g) whole kernel corn, drained
cooking oil
1 onion, finely chopped
100 g button mushrooms, sliced
1 packet (250 g) back bacon, fried and chopped
250 ml grated Cheddar cheese
45 ml cream or cream cheese

Samp tart

Preheat the oven to 180 °C. Grease a medium ovenproof dish. Drain the samp and cook in fresh water until soft. Season with salt. Heat the butter and fry the onion, bacon and mushrooms until done. Mix the remaining ingredients, add the bacon mixture and samp and spoon into the prepared dish. Bake in the preheated oven for 1 hour, or until firm and brown on top.

SERVES 6–8.

500 ml samp, soaked overnight
salt
10 ml butter
1 onion, chopped
1 packet (250 g) back bacon, chopped
200 g button mushrooms, sliced
250 ml mayonnaise
125 ml cream
1 packet (60 g) white onion soup powder
250 ml grated Cheddar cheese
freshly ground black pepper to taste

upside-down vegetable tart

The vegetables are stir-fried in a pan, covered with pastry and then baked in the oven.
When it comes out of the oven the tart is upturned so the vegetables are on top.

TOPPING

45 ml olive oil

2 leeks, sliced

1 red pepper, seeded and sliced
  into strips

150 g butternut, peeled and cubed

¼ small cauliflower or broccoli,
  broken into smaller florets

15 ml balsamic vinegar

45 ml grated Parmesan cheese

15 ml chopped fresh parsley

salt and freshly ground black
  pepper to taste

PASTRY

250 ml cake flour

250 ml self-raising flour

250 ml coarse mealie meal

5 ml paprika

150 g butter, diced

2 eggs, lightly whisked

Preheat the oven to 180 °C.

TOPPING: Heat the olive oil in a pan with an ovenproof handle and sauté the leeks, red pepper, butternut and cauliflower or broccoli over medium heat for 10 minutes. Remove from the heat and stir in the vinegar, Parmesan cheese, parsley, salt and pepper.

PASTRY: Mix the cake and self-raising flours, mealie meal and paprika. Rub the butter into the dry ingredients with your fingertips and, using a fork, stir in the whisked eggs. Roll out the pastry on a floured work surface until slightly bigger than the pan. Lay the pastry over the vegetables and gently press in along the inside of the rim of the pan. Bake in the preheated oven for 25–30 minutes, or until a testing skewer comes out clean. Leave the tart to cool in the pan for 5 minutes before upturning onto a serving platter. Serve hot. *[pg 191]*

SERVES 6–8.

VARIATION: Stir-fry vegetables such as mushrooms, sweet peppers and baby marrows with plenty of garlic until soft. Add a few cherry tomatoes and pitted black olives and crumble feta cheese on top before proceeding with the pastry. Use instead of the topping vegetables.

VARIATION: Instead of the vegetables, use 20 peeled pickling onions sautéed in 15 ml each olive oil and butter. Crumble 100 g blue cheese on top and cover with a layer of scone dough.

TIP: Leave the pan to rest on the upturned tart for a few minutes so the vegetables can sink onto the pastry crust without breaking or falling apart.

TIP: If you're in a hurry, use ready-made rolled-out puff pastry for the crust.

upside-down vegetable tart

'Braais are no longer informal get-togethers where you eat from paper plates, so we've included recipes for several stylish but easy desserts, such as tiramisu served in small cups, pavlova, fruit brûlée and, of course, trifle.'

sweet Temptations

Puddings for a braai should be quick and easy to make. Keep it simple and give old favourites new twists, such as char-grilled fruit instead of fruit salad, with semifreddo instead of ice cream. These days I'm also happy to serve biscotti or chocolate brownies with coffee or cheese in one form or another, especially now we have such a wide selection of cheeses from which to choose. When camping and you have to make do with basic cooking facilities, make a pudding over the coals — braai fruit or bake a pot pudding and enjoy it with ice cream or frozen yoghurt. Cake is also a sure winner, especially if it's cheesecake covered with lots of caramel.

ROASTED FRUIT

Roasted pineapple with coconut or ginger cream

Cut an unpeeled pineapple into quarters, core and all. Sprinkle with brown or icing sugar or brush with honey and braai rapidly over the coals until blackened in parts. Cut the flesh from the peel, but leave it inside the peel, and serve with one of the following:

COCONUT CREAM: Mix 250 ml cream or mascarpone or cottage cheese with 80 ml toasted desiccated coconut.

GINGER CREAM: Finely chop 45 ml ginger preserve and add to 250 ml cream or mascarpone or cream cheese with plenty of the syrup.

Roasted bananas with toffee sauce

Roast bananas in their peels over the coals until black on the outside. Peel and drizzle with toffee sauce.

TOFFEE SAUCE: Mix 50 g butter, 60 ml soft brown sugar, 45 ml golden syrup, 45 ml cream and 2 ml vanilla essence and heat until the sugar has melted and the sauce has thickened slightly. Stir frequently.

Roasted figs with chocolate

Cut a cross in the top of each fig and insert a square of dark chocolate in each opening. Grill over medium heat until the figs are hot and the chocolate has melted. Spoon thick Greek yoghurt, mascarpone cheese or crème fraîche into a bowl and drizzle with honey. Serve with the figs and biscotti.

VARIATION – AMARETTI WITH MASCARPONE: Roughly chop 50 g amaretti biscuits and mix with 250 g mascarpone cheese.

Roasted nectarines or plums

Halve the nectarines and sprinkle generously with brown sugar or castor sugar. Grill cut side down over the coals until caramelised. Sprinkle with flaked almonds and serve with mascarpone cheese or ice cream. *[pg 195]*

Roasted plums

Fruit fondue kebabs

KEBABS: Thread fruit – strawberries, nectarines and pineapple – onto skewers. Sprinkle with icing sugar. Grill over medium coals until lightly browned. *[pg 196]*

FRUIT SAUCE: Purée strawberries or mixed berries with a little castor sugar until smooth.

ORANGE AND CHOCOLATE SAUCE: Heat 15 ml cocoa powder, 150 ml orange juice, 15 ml golden syrup and 90 ml cream in a saucepan until slightly thickened.

CHOCOLATE SAUCE: Heat 200 g chocolate broken into squares with 250 ml cream. Stir continuously until the chocolate has melted completely. *[pg 196]*

YOGHURT AND CHOCOLATE SAUCE: For a healthier option, melt the chocolate slowly and stir in 250 ml thick Greek yoghurt.

TIP: Toast marshmallows over the fire and dip them in the chocolate sauce.

SERVING SUGGESTION 1: Put a pavlova (pg 198) on a plate for each guest and fill with yoghurt cream or ice cream. Serve with 1 or 2 fruit skewers and drizzle a little of the strawberry sauce on top.

SERVING SUGGESTION 2: Pour the chocolate sauce into small cups and serve with the fruit kebabs and biscotti.

Baked apple

Core 1 Granny Smith apple per person and grease with butter on the outside. Mix together raisins, chopped pecan nuts, brown sugar and a pinch of cinnamon and use to fill the apples. Put a knob of butter on top of the mixture and wrap individually in aluminium foil. Bake over cool coals for about 45 minutes until soft. Serve with cream or ice cream.

Fruit brûlée

Spoon fruit salad into ovenproof bowls and spoon a thick layer of ready-made custard and thick (not pouring) cream on top. Sprinkle with a generous layer of brown sugar and put under a heated grill until the sugar has melted. You can also use a chef's blowtorch to melt the sugar.

Millionaire's ice cream

Finely chop 100 g Brazil nuts, 100 g chocolate, 12 glacé cherries and 60 ml preserved fruit. Crush 1 packet (125 g) finger biscuits and fold into 2 litres bought ice cream along with the chocolate mixture. Freeze until needed.

Hot winter fruit salad

Arrange 1 kg winter fruit such as guava, apple, pear and orange slices in an ovenproof dish, sprinkle with 100 ml brown sugar and pour over 100 ml white wine or apple juice. Also add whole spices such as cinnamon and/or chopped fresh ginger and star anise. Bake for 20 minutes, or until the fruit is soft. Serve with custard yoghurt (below).

CUSTARD YOGHURT: Mix 250 ml ready-made custard with 250 ml vanilla yoghurt. Serve with the hot fruit salad.

Quick fruit tart

Brush 8 sheets of phyllo pastry with melted butter. Arrange on a greased baking sheet. Top with slices of fresh fruit such as nectarines, pineapple, apples, gooseberries, peaches or plums, leaving a 7 cm edge clear all around. Add cherries or berries if desired. Sprinkle the fruit with 30 ml castor sugar and flaked almonds and 1 ml ground cinnamon. Fold the pastry edges over the fruit and bake at 200 °C for 15–20 minutes, or until the pastry is crisp and lightly browned. Serve with ice cream. *[pg 197]*

Lemon cream tart

Brush 8 sheets of phyllo pastry with butter, arrange in layers in a greased 24 cm pie dish and bake at 200 °C for 10 minutes. Reduce oven temperature to 160 °C. Whisk 250 ml castor sugar, 4 extra-large eggs, 250 ml cream and 250 ml lemon juice and pour into the crust. Bake until the filling is firm. Dust lemon slices with icing sugar and heat over hot coals or under the oven grill until lightly browned. Stack on top of the cooked tart (or use sliced strawberries). Serve with ice cream.

Quick fresh fruitcake

Mix 310 ml cake flour, 5 ml baking powder, pinch salt and 180 ml sugar. Melt 125 g butter and whisk in 2 extra-large eggs. Add the butter mixture to the flour mixture and turn the batter into a greased 24 cm loose-bottomed tin. Spoon 4 x 250 ml summer fruit such as berries, strawberries, grapes and diced peaches on top, sprinkle with brown sugar and bake at 180 °C for 1 hour.

Semifreddo

Whisk together 4 extra-large egg yolks, 60 ml sugar and 10 ml vanilla essence. Whisk the egg whites until stiff, then fold into 500 ml whipped cream. Fold the cream mixture into the egg yolk mixture. Fold in 200 g chopped pistachio nuts, spoon the mixture into a bowl and freeze until firm. Serve with fruit.

ALL THE ABOVE DESSERTS SERVE UP TO 6.

Pavlova with summer berries

The toppings may change from time to time but pavlova is one of those classic desserts that will always be in demand. To this day it's still a sensational creation with flavours and textures that offset each other beautifully.

MERINGUE

4 extra-large egg whites
pinch salt
200 ml castor sugar (or use
    100 ml fine yellow sugar)
15 ml white vinegar
30 ml cornflour

FILLING

125 ml cream, stiffly whipped
125 ml Greek yoghurt
15 ml castor sugar
1 packet (250 g) frozen mixed
    summer berries
45 ml brown sugar
15 ml brandy
handful chopped toasted hazelnuts
fresh mint to decorate

Preheat the oven to 150 °C. Line a baking sheet with baking paper and dust with cornflour.

MERINGUE: Whisk the egg whites and salt until soft peaks form. Whisk in the castor sugar a little at a time. Whisk until the mixture is smooth and shiny. Using a metal spoon, fold in the vinegar and cornflour. Spoon the meringue mixture onto the prepared baking sheet, spreading it evenly to make a rectangular shape. Make a slight hollow in the centre. Bake in the preheated oven for 45–50 minutes, or until crisp on the outside but still soft inside. Leave the meringue on a wire rack to cool.

FILLING: Mix the stiffly whipped cream, the yoghurt and the castor sugar. Heat the berries, brown sugar and brandy until just warm. Fill the meringue shells with the cream mixture just before serving. Spoon the berries on top, sprinkle with the nuts and decorate with mint leaves. *[pg 199]*

SERVES 6–8.

VARIATION 1: Fill the meringue shell with ice cream and serve with roasted fresh figs (pg 194) or strawberries.

VARIATION 2: Arrange banana slices on the yoghurt cream and decorate with small spoonfuls of granadilla pulp.

VARIATION 3: Buy crisp meringues, break into pieces and arrange alternating layers of crushed meringue, fruit and yoghurt cream in tall glasses. Sprinkle with chopped nuts.

VARIATION 4: Make a chocolate fruit bowl. Spread melted chocolate on the base and sides of a loose-bottomed cake tin and leave to set in the fridge. Carefully remove the chocolate shell from the tin and fill with yoghurt cream and fruit.

HINT: You can also make smaller meringues and serve them individually.

Pavlova with summer berries

Berry trifle

For a healthier option, use a mixture of cream cheese and yoghurt instead of cream.

1 packet (80 g) strawberry jelly
250 ml boiling water
125 ml dessert wine or cold water
15 ml lemon juice
250 ml frozen mixed berries
1 chocolate swiss roll, sliced
50 ml sherry or brandy (optional)
1 tub (250 g) cream cheese
80–100 ml plain yoghurt
20 ml castor sugar
250 g strawberries, washed, hulled
    and halved
500 ml ready-made custard
100 g almonds or pecan nuts,
    toasted

Dissolve the jelly powder in the boiling water. Add the dessert wine or cold water, lemon juice and berries and chill until set. Arrange a layer of cake in the bottom of a large glass bowl and sprinkle with the sherry or brandy if desired. Mix the cream cheese, yoghurt and sugar. Layer all the ingredients, including the jelly, in the bowl, including layers of custard and strawberries, starting with the cake and ending with a cream cheese layer. Sprinkle the nuts on top.

SERVES 6–8.

VARIATION 1: Omit the sugar and add 1 can (360 g) caramel condensed milk and 125 ml lemon juice to the cream cheese mixture.

VARIATION 2 – QUICK TRIFLE: Layer swiss roll, sponge cake or sponge fingers, fresh or frozen berries and strawberries and the cream cheese mixture in tall glasses and sprinkle with toasted chopped almonds.

VARIATION 3: Use caramel condensed milk or chocolate sauce instead of the cream cheese mixture.

VARIATION 4: Use ginger and green fig preserves and chopped glacé fruit instead of fresh fruit, and add pieces of chocolate.

Potjie brown pudding

SYRUP
500 ml water
250 ml sugar
5 ml vanilla essence
25 ml lemon juice

BATTER
60 g butter or margarine
375 ml cake flour
3 ml ground cinnamon
3 ml ground ginger
60 ml sugar
125 ml apricot jam
60 ml milk
5 ml bicarbonate of soda
7 ml vinegar or lemon juice

SYRUP: Heat together all the syrup ingredients, stirring until the sugar has dissolved. Simmer for 5 minutes.

BATTER: Rub the butter or margarine into the cake flour. Add the spices, sugar and jam. Mix the milk, bicarbonate of soda and vinegar or lemon juice with the flour mixture.

Spoon the batter into the boiling syrup, cover and simmer for 15–20 minutes or until done. Serve with a little evaporated milk, custard or cream.

SERVES 6.

Marmalade roly-poly

Andries Krogman, potjiekos king, likes to make a roly-poly pudding in a potjie. For a change, spread the dough with marmalade instead of apricot jam and make the syrup with orange juice.

DOUGH: Sift together the cake flour and baking powder and rub in the butter. Add the eggs and milk and mix to make a stiff dough. Roll out the dough thinly on a floured surface. Spread with marmalade and roll up. Cut the dough roll into slices.

SAUCE: Mix all the sauce ingredients in a flat-bottomed potjie and boil for 2 minutes. Arrange the dough slices in the pot, laying them flat. Cover with the lid and bake over cool coals for about 45 minutes, or until the dough is done. Put some coals on the lid of the pot (more here than under the pot). Serve the roly-poly with custard.

SERVES 6.

TIP: Bake the pudding in a preheated oven at 180 °C for 30–40 minutes until done.

DOUGH
500 ml cake flour
10 ml baking powder
125 g butter
2 extra-large eggs, whisked
± 30 ml milk
marmalade

SAUCE
500 ml fresh orange juice
250 ml sugar
45 ml butter
80 ml orange liqueur (optional)
finely grated zest of 1 orange

Chocolate mocha pudding

This deliciously moist, coffee-flavoured chocolate pudding requires very little mixing.

Preheat the oven to 180 °C. Grease a deep ovenproof dish.

BATTER: Break the egg into a measuring jug and add enough milk to make up 125 ml. Add the remaining batter ingredients, except the brown sugar and pecan nuts, and beat well. Spoon the batter into the dish and sprinkle over the sugar and nuts.

SAUCE: Mix all the ingredients and pour the sauce over the batter. Bake in the preheated oven for 30–45 minutes, or until done. Serve with ice cream.

SERVES 6.

TIP: You can also make the pudding in a potjie. Prepare as described, spoon the batter into a greased flat-bottomed potjie and cover with the lid. Bake over cool coals (also put coals on top of the lid).

BATTER
1 extra-large egg
milk
250 ml self-raising flour
pinch salt
60 ml cocoa powder
25 ml instant coffee granules
160 ml castor sugar
125 ml brown sugar
125 ml chopped pecan nuts

SAUCE
300 ml hot strong coffee
60 ml cocoa powder
125 ml castor sugar

Tiramisu cups

This tiramisu recipe is healthier than the traditional version made with mascarpone cheese.
Make individual desserts in small coffee cups or freeze like ice cream (see variation).

15 ml strong instant coffee granules
60 ml boiling water
45 ml coffee liqueur
2 eggs, separated
45 ml castor sugar
1 tub (250 g) cream cheese
1 tub (250 g) smooth cottage cheese
   or plain yoghurt
1 packet (125 g) finger biscuits
125 ml grated chocolate (optional)
cocoa powder for dusting

Dissolve the coffee granules in the boiling water, add the liqueur and leave to cool. Whisk together the egg yolks and castor sugar until pale. Add the cream cheese and cottage cheese or yoghurt and mix well. Whisk the egg whites until stiff and fold into the egg yolk mixture. Dip the biscuits into the cooled coffee, break into pieces and layer them in the bottom of each cup. Spoon a little of the cheese mixture on top. Top with a sprinkling of grated chocolate if desired. Repeat the layers, ending with the cheese mixture. Dust each cup with cocoa powder and chill until firm, preferably overnight. They will keep well in the fridge for 2 days.

MAKES 8–12 CUPS.

VARIATION: Layer the ingredients in a loaf tin lined with clingfilm, ending with a layer of biscuits. Cover tightly with the clingfilm and freeze until firm. Unmould the tiramisu and serve sliced, with fresh berries.

Caramel cheesecake

CRUST
125 g butter
30 ml castor sugar
30 ml cooking oil
1 extra-large egg
500 ml cake flour
10 ml baking powder
2 ml salt

FILLING
4 extra-large eggs
150–250 ml sugar
1 ml salt
juice and zest of 1 lemon or
   60 ml lemon juice
2 tubs (250 g each) smooth
   cottage cheese
2 tubs (250 g each) creamed
   cottage cheese or cream cheese
100 ml cake flour
1 can (360 g) caramel condensed
   milk

Preheat the oven to 160 °C. Grease a 23 cm loose-bottomed tin.

CRUST: Cream together the butter and castor sugar until pale. Add the oil and egg, beating well. Sift together the dry ingredients and add to the creamed mixture. Press the dough onto the base and against the sides of the prepared tin. Chill.

FILLING: Whisk together the eggs, sugar and salt until pale and thick. Add the lemon juice and zest, beating continuously. Add the smooth cottage cheese, creamed cottage cheese or cream cheese and flour and mix well. Turn the mixture into the prepared crust and bake in the preheated oven for 45–60 minutes, or until the filling has set. Switch off the oven and leave the cheesecake to cool in the oven. Unmould onto a plate and spread the caramel condensed milk on top. Caramelise slightly with a chef's blowtorch.

MAKES 1 LARGE CHEESECAKE.

TIP: Replace the crust with a crumb crust made from crushed Tennis biscuits mixed with melted butter.

Cheesecake brûlée

You can make these crustless individual cheesecakes in a jiffy. The filling is made with amasi (sour milk) instead of cream so the fat content is much lower. The hard, caramelised sugar layer makes it special, but you can also omit it.

Preheat the oven to 160 °C. Grease 6 dariole moulds or ramekins with butter.

CAKE: Mix the cream cheese and castor sugar with a wooden spoon. Add the eggs, one by one, beating until well blended. Add the lemon juice and finally fold in the sour milk. Spoon the mixture into the prepared moulds and put in an oven pan filled with water. Bake in the preheated oven for 30–40 minutes, or until firm. Cool to room temperature before refrigerating.

BRÛLÉE: Sprinkle the sugar over the chilled cheesecakes and heat under the oven grill until the sugar is just caramelised. Alternatively, use a chef's blowtorch.

MAKES 6 CHEESECAKES.

CAKE

2 tubs (250 g each) cream cheese
180 ml castor sugar
3 extra-large eggs
50 ml lemon juice
250 ml sour milk

BRÛLÉE LAYER

80 ml castor sugar

Festive fruitcake loaf

This light fruitcake, which basically consists of dried fruit and nuts only, is completely different to the traditional heavy, dark, spiced Christmas cake and can be made any day of the year, no matter what the occasion.

Preheat the oven to 150 °C. Grease a medium loaf tin and line with baking paper. Grease again.

Combine the fruit and nuts. Sift the cake flour, baking powder and salt on top and mix. Whisk together the eggs, honey and essences and fold the mixture into the fruit mixture. Turn the batter into the prepared tin, spreading it evenly. Bake in the preheated oven for about 1½ hours, or until done and firm. Take care the cake doesn't burn on the sides. Leave the cake to cool in the tin, turn out and remove the baking paper. Sprinkle with brandy, wrap the cake in aluminium foil and store in an airtight container. The cake will keep like this for 3 months.

To serve, cut the cake into very thin slices and arrange on a cheese platter along with a selection of cheeses, such as Parmesan cheese, blue cheese and soft cream cheese. Serve with port or sherry.

MAKES 1 MEDIUM LOAF CAKE.

60–125 g dried apricots, chopped
200 g whole red glacé cherries
100 g candied citrus peel
125 ml sultanas
125 ml chopped dates or currants
100 g Brazil nuts, roughly chopped
100 g blanched almonds, roughly chopped
100 g pecan nuts, roughly chopped
100 g ground almonds
100 ml cake flour
2 ml baking powder
pinch salt
3 extra-large eggs
30 ml honey
10 ml vanilla essence
2–3 drops almond essence
brandy

Baked camembert with fresh figs

CHEESE FOR DESSERT

Set out a platter of cheeses with crackers or biscotti, as well as fresh fruit, poached summer berries [pg 205, centre] or fruit preserves. Soft cheeses such as Brie and Camembert, as well as mascarpone, goat cheese, cream cheese and blue cheese also provide a good finish to a meal. You can also serve slices of fruitcake with matured Cheddar or Parmesan cheese shavings.

Baked Camembert

Camembert stuffed with green fig preserve and nuts is delicious if baked in the oven for 5 minutes.

Preheat the oven to 160 °C. Slice the Camembert horizontally through the middle and layer the cream cheese, blue cheese and half the nuts and green fig preserve on the bottom half of the cheese. Cover with the other half, drizzle with honey and pile the remaining nuts and green fig preserve on top. Place on a baking sheet and bake in the preheated oven for 5 minutes. Serve immediately.

1 round firm, unripe Camembert
250 g cream cheese
100 g blue cheese (optional)
chopped walnuts or pecan nuts
sliced green fig preserve
honey

VARIATION 1: Spoon a few teaspoons of honey over the Camembert and bake at 160 °C for 5 minutes. Serve with fresh grapes or figs and slices of oven-dried pears and apples if preferred. *[pg 204]*

VARIATION 2: Stew mixed dried fruit (500 g in total), such as apricots, sultanas, cranberries, raisins and currants, in a syrup of 125 ml water, 60 ml sugar, 125 ml orange juice or white wine, 90 ml sherry, 1 stick cinnamon, and a piece of orange peel or a vanilla pod, until soft. Serve with Camembert cheese. *[pg 205, right]*

VARIATION 3: Boil 500 g mixed glazed fruit in 350 ml Van der Hum liqueur until

Index

A

achar
  mango 90
  Thai 93
Africa
  bean salad 177
  chicken with chickpea stew 118
  salad dressing 165
  vegetable pot 183
  venison potjie 53
antipasti 21
apple, baked 196

B

bananas, roasted with toffee
  sauce 194
basting sauce
  apricot 94
  soy sauce 106
  sweet 'n sour 106
beans, texas 80
beef fillet
  avocado 29
  wagon wheels 29
  with berry sauce 31
  with chocolate and chilli sauce 31
  with feta cheese and spinach
    stuffing 32
  Witsand-Kalahari 28
beetroot chips 39
berry trifle 200
boerewors
  and bean salad 101
  breakfast surprise 101
  couscous delight 101
  nibbles 100
boerewors rolls
  gourmet 100
  tortilla 100
braai guide
  chicken 104
  fish and seafood 126
  lamb 72

pork 56
steak 27
venison 27, 42
braai pap tart 189
braai sauce
  chutney and tomato 11
  marmalade 123
  sweet 'n sour 123
bread
  anchovy and cheese 152
  bruschetta, basic 22
  cheese and onion flat 160
  ciabatta with caramelised tomato
    and Camembert 22
  flat ash 160
  grape loaf 159
  lavache 153
  olive flat 160
  picnic loaf 152
  pot 158
  pot, with tomato and
    cheese-cream sauce 159
  pumpkin seed loaf 157
  quick mealie meal loaf 154
  raisin loaf 154
  seed loaf 157
  sourdough bread, toasted, with
    nutty mushrooms 22
  steamed mealie meal loaf 153
  sweet coconut loaf 153
bread bake, savoury 22
bread dough, basic 158
bread for burgers 98
bread tart 188
breakfast boerewors surprise 101
brinjal
  marinated 20
  roasted 19
  roasted, with stuffing 180
burgers
  bread for 98
  cheese 98
  chicken 99

econo- 98
extras 99
fish 99
gourmet 98
spicy 98
butter for steak
  anchovy 35
  blue cheese 34
  feta cheese and herb 34
  herb 34
butternut
  chips 39
  with spinach or mealie stuffing 181

C

calamari
  char-grilled steaks 132
  fried 18
  risotto 133
  stuffed 132
Camdeboo Karoo Venison 42
Camembert, baked 205
cheese and tomato sticks 23
cheesecake (sweet)
  brûlée 203
  caramel 202
cheesecake (savoury)
  savoury 188
  spinach 188
chermoula 13
chicken
  braaied Greek 106
  butterflied 116
  butterflied, with fragrant butter 118
  camp site 109
  curry 105
  espetadas 93
  in a clay pot in the ground 111
  lemon and herb 120
  mayonnaise 108
  mustard 110
  nuggets 18
  salad 105

stuffing for pita breads 106
tandoori 111
Thai 110
with chickpea stew, Africa 118
chicken breasts
  Cajun 114
  Eastern 115
  Mexican 114
  spicy 115
  with cheese stuffing 115
chicken liver and bacon rolls 18
chicken skewers
  dukkah 90
  satay 92
chicken wings
  Chinese 113
  sticky 113
  sweet 'n sour 18
  sweet chilli and tomato 113
chickpea
  chorizo stew 119
  sauce 95
  stew 119
chimichurri 14
ciabatta with caramelised tomato
  and Camembert 22
couscous delight 101
crayfish with lemon butter 134

D

dessert
  bananas, roasted with toffee
    sauce 194
  caramel cheesecake 202
  chocolate mocha pudding 201
  fruit brûlée 196
  fruitcake, quick fresh 197
  fruitcake with cheese, festive 203
  fruit kebabs, fondue 196
  fruit salad, hot winter 196
  fruit tart, quick 197
  ice cream, millionaire's 196
  lemon cream tart 197

pudding, brown potjie 200
roly-poly, marmalade 201
semifreddo 197
tiramisu cups 202
trifle, berry 200
dessert sauce
chocolate 196
fruit 196
orange and chocolate 196
yoghurt and chocolate 196
Doms, Di 33
Drake, Justine 138
dukkah chicken skewers 90
du Plessis, Anton 44
du Toit, Piet 122

E

Engelbrecht, Elsabé 47
espetadas 93

F

February, Sharon 138
feta cheese
and sweet melon sticks 23
marinated 20
figs, roasted 194
with Amaretti-mascarpone 194
fish
chermoula 136
Thai 138
whole braaied 134, 135
with herb and spice butter 135
with red curry and coconut milk
sauce 136
fish fillets/portions
Cajun 141
in foil, Mediterrranean 145
marinated 145
pan-fried with rocket salsa 142
pan-fried with spicy tomato
sauce 142
skottel 141
with dukkah crust 144
with grilled lemon halves 144
fish potjie, curried 146
fish stew, Moroccan 146
Friis, Naomi 157
fruit brûlée 196
fruitcake
quick fresh 197
with cheese, festive 203
fruit kebabs, fondue 196
fruit salad, hot winter 196
fruit tart, quick 197

G

garlic bulbs, roasted 179
gemsbok marrowbone potjie,
Kalahari 52

Giggling Gourmet 89
gremolata 52
guacamole 83

H

halloumi, fried 19
harders with coriander and
chilli sauce 140
harissa 13
hummus 95

I

ice cream, millionaire's 196
Institute of Culinary Arts 121

J

Jemima's in Oudtshoorn 90

K

kebabs
chicken 97
pork 97
seafood 97
Kgalagadi Transfrontier Park 44
kofta 94
Krogman, Andries 201

L

Lady Laatvy 44
lamb
creamy spiced 80
pot, Greek 76
lamb, chops
Mediterranean 73
stuffed 73
with cheese topping 73
lamb, leg
braaied 75
butterflied 75
Greek 76
Mexican 83
Moroccan 85
royal 85
lamb, shoulder
braaied 75
Turkish 80
lamb roll, Mediterranean 81
Langberg Guest Lodge 89
lavache 152
lemon cream tart 197
Le Must restaurant 32

M

Mama Africa restaurant 53
mango achar 90
Margolius, Marcia 152, 168
marinades
basic 9
Cajun 10

Chinese 10
citrus 9
mustard 9
rosemary 9
spicy yoghurt 10
versatile curry 11
wine 11
marinade for chicken
basic 9
curry-yoghurt 105
Greek 106
tandoori 111
teriyaki 123
Thai 110
marinade for espetadas 93
marinade for kebabs
soy sauce and honey 96
Thai 96
marinade for lamb, basic 9
marinade for lamb, chops, basic 73
marinade for lamb, leg
basic 75
buttermilk 75
Mexican 83
royal 84
marinade for lamb, shoulder,
Turkish 80
marinade for pork
basic 9, 58
honey and soy sauce 63
rooibos 62
marinade for sosaties
best 88
Jenny's pork 89
yoghurt 88
marinade for steak
blue cheese 33
soy sauce 33
marinade for venison
buttermilk 48
herb 48
red wine and buttermilk 48
Matumi Game Lodge 42
mayonnaise, basil 90
mealie meal dumplings 28
mealies, whole 179
Melissa's 90, 118
meringue for pavlova 198
Morris, Jenny 89
Muisbosskerm 135
mullet
butterflied 140
with coriander and chilli sauce 140
Murphy, Sandra 37
mushrooms
marinated 20
stuffed with feta cheese and
pesto 20
with cheese filling 181

mussels
braaied 19
in the shell, garlic 127
in wine and cream sauce 128
pot 127
pot, Thai curry 128
mutton rib, stuffed herbed 84

N

nectarines, roasted 194
Neethling, Tini 89
nuts, spicy toasted 23

O

olives with tomato, Italian 21
onion rings, fried 39
onions
braised 100
caramelised 160

P

Paarman, Ina 33, 116
paella 147
pap tart, braai 189
pastes and spreads
chermoula 13
for pork, smoked paprika and
herb 66
for smoked pork chops 61
for steak, mustard 33
harissa 13
pavlova with summer berries 198
peanut (satay) sauce 93
peppers
roasted 167, 180
with couscous stuffing 181
pesto
coriander 14
feta, almond and paprika 14
Pick 'n Pay cookery school 80
Pieterse, Pieter 141
pineapple
roasted, with coconut cream 194
roasted, with ginger cream 194
pizza, quick pan 157
pork, chops
mustard 57
smoked 61
stuffed 60
sweet 'n sour 57
pork kebabs, satay 92
pork, leg
Italian 66
smoked 68
pork, loin, Mediterranean 66
pork, neck
orange and mustard 58
with fillet and blue cheese
stuffing 65

pork, spareribs
  eastern 63
  with rooibos marinade 62
pork, spicy 58
pork, steaks, orange and mustard 58
potatoes
  cake 186
  delicious mashed 185
  kebabs 182
  mayonnaise 185
  on the coals 179
  skewered wedges 182
  skottel braai 186
  stuffings for 179
potjie
  Africa vegetable 183
  Africa venison 53
  curried fish 146
  Greek lamb 76
  Kalahari gemsbok marrowbone 52
  mussel 127
  Thair curry mussel 128
  tomato and vegetable 183
prawns 18
  grilled garlic 130
  how to remove the alimentary
    canal 131
  in tomato sauce 131
  peri-peri 131
Prinsloo, Laetitia 121
pudding, brown potjie 200
pumpkin
  pie, sweet 189
  whole roasted 186

Q
quails
  in vine leaves 121
  orange and ginger 121

R
Reuben's Restaurant 62
Riffel, Reuben 62, 133
roly-poly, marmalade 201
rub
  braai 12
  lemon and herb 12
  Moroccan 12
  Texas 12
rump steak with tomato and
  feta cheese 32
rye bread, toasted, with pesto
  and cheese 22

S
salad
  Africa bean 177
  American potato 170
  Avocado and orange 169

beetroot 168
bowls 19
broccoli 168
brown rice 175
Chickpea and butternut 172
crushed wheat 174
Curried potato 170
Eastern noodle 177
Greek pasta 175
green, with toasted seeds 166
marinated vegetable and bean 174
Mediterranean 167
Mediterranean couscous 174
Mediterranean potato 167
quick chickpea 172
quick pasta 175
red cabbage and apple 169
sweet 'n sour cucumber 169
sweet melon 171
salad dressing
  Africa 165
  Eastern 165
  mayonnaise and yoghurt 166
  Mediterranean 165
salsa
  avocado 97
  cucumber 97
  gooseberry 29
  red pepper 136
  tomato 114
samp tart 189
sauce
  Argentinian parsley 14
  satay 93
sauce for chicken
  mayonnaise 108
  mustard 110
  peri-peri 123
sauce for pork
  anchovy 66
  apple 62
  easy mustard 68
  lemon and honey 57
  nutty red wine 65
  orange and mustard 58
  pineapple and mustard 61
  quick fruit 61
sauce for seafood, tartare 132
sauce for steak
  berry 31
  blue cheese 37
  champion mushroom 36
  chicken liver 37
  chocolate and chilli 31
  garlic 36
  green peppercorn 37
  mock mustard 37
  mushroom and wine 36
  mussel 36

sauce for venison
  bacon and mushroom 50
  cranberry 51
  green peppercorn 50
  pinotage 51
  port 51
  sour 50
Schippel, Pamela 80
semifreddo 197
sirloin steak, camembert 32
skilpadjies 47
snoek
  West Coast 138
  with apricot jam sauce 138
  with ginger and honey sauce 138
  with mayonnaise sauce 138
sosaties
  best 88
  curried chicken 90
  Jenny's pork 89
  Langberg venison 89
spice mixture
  Cajun 13
  for pork 58
  Indonesian 13
Spookhuis, Die 141
springbok, leg
  deboned 43
  Kalahari 43
springbok, loin, Kalahari 43
spring chickens, orange and
  ginger 121
Stadler, Llewellyn and Mariaan 44, 52
steak, camembert sirloin 32
sticks
  cheese and tomato 23
  feta cheese and sweet melon 23
Stoffberg, Myra 138
stuffing for lamb
  Moroccan 85
  royal 85
stuffing for mutton rib 85
stuffing for pork, blue cheese 65
stuffing for pork chops
  cheese 60
  vegetable 29
stuffing for steak, feta cheese and
  spinach 32
sweet potatoes on the coals 179

T
tandoori chicken 111
tapas 18
tartlets
  with cream cheese and olive
    topping 23
  with salami and cheese topping 23
  with sun-dried tomato and feta
    cheese topping 23

with tapenade and tomato
    topping 23
Thai
  achar 93
  chicken 110
  chicken burgers 99
  curry mussel pot 128
  fish 138
  fish burgers 99
  marinade 96
tiramisu cups 202
tomatoes
  and vegetable pot 183
  caramelised 32
  roasted 19
trifle, berry 200
turkey
  whole in the kettle braai 122
  with lemon-macadamia butter 122
  with orange-mustard glaze 122

V
van der Merwe, Daleen 43
van der Merwe, Elbé 43
van Hoogstraten, Melissa 90,
  118, 166
van Niekerk, Bertus 28
van Niekerk, Marchel 85
van Schalkwyk, Patricia 138
vegetables
  and cheese kebabs 182
  and cheese, char-grilled 178
  parcels 181
  pie with phyllo pastry 187
  pot, african 183
  stuffed 181
  tomato pot 183
  upside-down tart 190
venison back fillet, stuffed 43
venison fillet
  in bacon 42
  in caul 42
  matumi, with cheese 42
venison loin, Namibian stuffed 46
venison potjie, Africa 53
venison sausage, sosatie 47
vinaigrette
  basic 164
  herb 164
  mustard 164
von Schouroth, Erich & Zelda 46

W
West Coast snoek 138
Witsand Nature Reserve 28,110

Y
Yellowwood Café 37
yoghurt custard 197